10,000 Words an Hour

How to Use AI Tools like ChatGPT to Write Fiction Better and Faster, Without Increasing Writing Fatigue

Jason Hamilton

Myth HQ, LLC

CONTENTS

FREE Bonus!

By purchasing this book, you can gain access to my "AI Foundations Course" containing demonstrations of these techniques, plus dozens of story-generating prompts in my prompt library.

As an added bonus, you'll receive "The Plot Module Cheat Sheet" - a guide to crafting the perfect plot, chapter by chapter.

You can get these by signing up for my free community at https://nerdynovelist.com/free or using the QR code below.

1

How I Learned to Stop Worrying and Love the AI Overlords

My hands hovered over the keyboard, suspended, ready, anxious.

But completely unable to write.

This was back in 2019. I had been married for less than a year, and in that year I had recently published my tenth novel. For perspective, I published my first novel in 2018, just one year earlier.

And now I couldn't write to save my life. I did not know what was going on, why I was feeling this way, although in hindsight it seems rather obvious.

But before when I wrote it felt like escapism, like I was going to another world to explore the stories that happen there. Now it just felt like a chore.

I just could not write.

My wife and I are religious people, and at one point my wife asked me if maybe this was a sign, a sign from God that I wasn't meant to continue writing. Perhaps there was something else that was my calling, and I just hadn't found it yet.

Now, just so everyone knows, my wife was and continues to be my biggest fan, and has never ceased to encourage me throughout my entire author journey. So for her to even mention something like that was a big deal.

I gave this thought some serious reflection. Maybe she was right. Maybe this was a sign, if not from God, then maybe from my inner psyche, that perhaps the life of an author was not for me. It was a scary thought, given that I had devoted hundreds of hours over the last two years to creating stories that had been in my head for over a decade already. And I had so many more.

But let me give you a bit of backstory.

At this time, I was currently writing the third book in a six-book series. The first two had just come out, one right after another. I had high expectations for these books. Not only were they far better quality than my first series (of which I wrote eight books), but my marketing game was on point. I was doing everything all of the self-publishing gurus tell you to do. I had an email list, a launch plan, a lineup of book promotions, a blog tour, and a great cover and book description (both of which I paid for). I even took out a small personal loan so I could have money for Facebook and Amazon ads. I was that sure of this series' success.

Quick tip: don't do that.

I released both books within a week of each other as I finished up writing the third book.

And both bombed, horrifically.

I spent over $1000 on ad spend before I turned the ads off. My books had made less than half that. All the tips and tricks I had learned to "game the Amazon algorithm" and get more readers had completely failed me. And somehow, my second book series, even with a larger email list and more experience as a self-publisher, ended up performing far worse than my first book series a year earlier.

It was heartbreaking.

What I didn't know then, but is obvious to me now, was that I was experiencing a classic case of burnout, which often comes when you work very hard with no perceived compensation.

Side note: the word "perceived" is very intentional. Often, burnout just comes because we have unrealistic expectations, as I did. If you keep your expectations low, and find compensation/fulfillment in something more within your control (like improving as an author), you might circumvent burnout. I hit it hard because I tied my fulfillment to money, so when I didn't receive any, I burned out fast.

Side side note: read Becca Syme's book on burnout, Dear Writer, Are You in Burn Out? It's fantastic.

Thankfully, I didn't quit the writing game, despite my wife's concern. I knew that writing, content creation, and storytelling were the things that brought me the most ful-fillment.

I eventually finished book 3, and even book 4, but it took me over a year for each of them, when I had previously written 10 books in 2 years.

And other things began to happen in my life, thankfully in a (mostly) positive direction. I had my first child in January of 2021, just as COVID restrictions were starting to ease. She became the second love of my life.

Then, about six months later, I got my dream job working as the content manager for Kindlepreneur, one of the leading websites out there for self-published authors.

That meant that I was writing again, but I was mostly writing nonfiction FOR authors instead of my own fiction.

Only two months after that, my wife and I moved to coastal North Carolina, within just a few blocks of the water.

Life was looking pretty good.

But I still had a lot of trouble writing my fiction.

And that was when ChatGPT exploded on the scene.

I had played around with AI before, and once ChatGPT became a big thing, I gave it another try.

I experimented first with nonfiction, writing a few articles for my own website. In a single day, I wrote 16,000 words, more than I had ever done before, more than I even usually wrote in a week.

Then a few months later, OpenAI, the company behind ChatGPT, released GPT-4, the newly updated model, and I realized that AI was finally in a place where it could coherently write fiction.

So I experimented.

It was glorious.

And I began to write again.

My obsession with AI eventually led me to start a YouTube channel (The Nerdy Novelist) for fiction authors who want to use AI. I documented my process and progress as I started writing fiction in earnest again. That YouTube channel began to really gain some traction and is, as of this writing, the biggest AI YouTube channel for fiction writers.

AI has allowed me to get back into the game of writing fiction, in a way that I wouldn't have thought possible not too long ago.

The real reason I started that YouTube channel, and am writing this book now, is because I know that what I've discovered can help other authors like me, authors (or potential authors) who are crippled in their writing.

Through the YouTube channel, I've now met tons of authors who found my videos and told me that AI, along with my instruction, is what allowed them to write their first book, or to push through burnout, ADHD, dyslexia, being on the autism spectrum, and more. These are all things that make it difficult to write in the traditional way.

That is why I ultimately wrote this book, because I've seen what AI can do to help those who have struggled. It helped me, it has helped thousands of others, and it can help you too.

It can help you to finally get your first book idea on paper. It can help you write with debilitating illness or chronic struggles. It can help you write more, so you can get all of those fantastic ideas out into the world without having to hire a team of ghostwriters to do so. It can ease your writing fatigue by severely reducing the number of tiny decisions that writers have to make with each sentence that they write.

Whether you fall into one of those categories (Dyslexic, ADHD, on the spectrum, burnout, brain fog, etc.) or whether you're just interested in learning how AI can help you write faster, write better, and save you a lot of headache, this book is the master guide on this subject.

In the end, it's my goal to get you to write your first book, or, if you're already an established writer, to break past any barriers you have and be more productive.

If you're skeptical, don't just take my word for it. Here are some actual messages I've received from people who have found value from the principles that I will teach you in this book (some of the names have been changed for privacy):

This first one is from Jason:

"You are the reason I was able to write my first novel. At first, I just thought it'd be cool if a robot could write my story idea. I didn't know anything about creative writing, and only the basics of writing in general. I found out pretty quick that it was going to take more than telling the robomonkey to dance for me to get my idea into a book. Tons of useless deadend YouTube videos later, I find your channel.

"Your approaches, your prompts, your recommendations, your practices. An entirely new world opened up for me, and for that, regardless of whatever happens with your numbers on YouTube, you will always be the most valuable resource on the subject for me. So, even though it's nowhere near enough from me to give in return, thank you."

And this from Rob:

"I just wanted to thank you for your content on YouTube. I've always wanted to write, to tell stories, and although I have hundreds of ideas written down, thanks to a near fatal illness, I haven't been able to get words out of my head and onto the page.

"That was until I came across your AI content on YouTube. Thanks to your videos, I've gone from empty page (empty head) to a complete first draft of a short, pulp story. I know it's not much, but it's something I've never been able to do before. You've helped me get the story out of my head and onto the page with the help of AI and your techniques. I don't think I could have done it without your help."

And finally, this from Emily:

"My 8 year old daughter who is also AuDHD (and super struggles with reading) has written 2 books with me and AI helping her that she was able to give to her teachers at the end of the year...which meant an extra lot to them because they know how hard she has to work at all of this...they wouldn't have been made at all without AI and your help! So, anyway, all this to say: thank you for taking the time to put together all the resources you've shared."

It's for reasons like this that I keep going, and that I'm writing this book now. I hope you will also find a lot of useful information in these pages.

2

SETTING EXPECTATIONS

B efore we go any further, I'd like to set a few expectations about what this book will cover, and what it won't.

Because with any discussion of Artificial Intelligence, there are a million different paths that we could follow.

First, let me start by telling you what this book will not cover:

1. This book is not going to dig deep into the ethics or legal cases surrounding AI.

These are insanely complicated topics, and while I am no expert in law or ethics, I have read a lot of takes from those who are, enough to know that there are intelligent people debating copyright, and whether it's okay for an AI to be trained on the copyrighted work of an author.

From everything I've researched, it looks like there isn't a good legal case against AI, and so nothing is likely to change about what AI is permitted to do, although we may see some legislation or standard practices that lead to companies seeking permission from copyright holders in order to train their models on their work.

The problem is that this will likely be too little too late, for those who are hoping such legislation will close the door on AI. Already, we're seeing smaller language models hit the market, meaning that very soon, anyone with a laptop will be able to use these smaller language models and train them on their own data.

The genie really is out of the bottle, and while it's maybe not a nice thing that these companies trained the models on copyrighted material, it was almost certainly legal. And given the fact that mega-corporations like Disney or Warner Brothers haven't sued any of these AI companies yet (knowing full well that the models were trained on their intellectual property), is a good sign that their massive legal teams know they wouldn't have a case.

That's the legal side. The ethical side is a little harder to come to an agreement on. And while we can debate ethics endlessly, I am choosing not to do so. I have seen lives change, people who have wanted to write a book for years and couldn't, suddenly find themselves bringing their ideas to life because of AI.

AI has allowed a previously underprivileged group (and yes, being in a position to write a full-length novel with no outside help is a privilege), to finally have the opportunity they need.

Yes, AI has some scary implications for the future. I believe everybody, whether they use AI or not, should have a healthy fear of AI. But I also believe that the best way to control that fear and hedge our bets against the future is to embrace learning.

And since you are reading this book, I'm guessing that's exactly what you want to do.

Now for those who DO want me to go deeper on these topics, I have addressed many of the concerns that I get about AI in the back of this book. As I said, I'm no lawyer, but I've done my best to address most of the common concerns about AI. However, that content is more for your information, and not necessarily the "meat" of what this book is about, and I'm sure that for most of you I will be preaching to the choir, but I felt it was my due diligence to at least make an attempt to cover what I could.

2. This book will not tell you how to set up your ChatGPT account

Too many of the books I've read have entire chapters about the technical steps to get started with ChatGPT. It feels almost like the authors just wanted to pad the book out.

First off, the world of AI is changing so rapidly, and in a (probably hopeless) attempt to keep this book as evergreen as possible, I'm not going to tell you how to set up your ChatGPT/Claude/Gemini/etc. account, type your first prompt, etc.

In fact, I'm betting most of you have already done this, or at the very least have the minimal computer skills to figure it out and would skip such a chapter anyway.

And if you do need help, feel free to look it up. Most of these tools have great documentation, and a simple Google search should tell you exactly what to do. I've also created several videos on my YouTube channel to address challenges like these.

3. This book does not cover nonfiction

While I have written a lot of nonfiction, and will probably write another book on that subject in the future, that is not what this book is about.

This book is specifically for writing fiction with AI, and it's a comprehensive guide for doing so.

So, what is this book about and who is it for?

This book is about writing fiction with AI. Period, full stop.

Specifically, I'm going to tell you how to write faster and write better, using tools like ChatGPT and Claude (as well as a few others)

We're going to talk about a lot of things that I'm very excited to share with you. We'll cover some specific prompts and frameworks that I recommend you use when creating with AI. We're going to discuss what actually makes a good book, so you will know how to steer these Large Language Models in that direction. We're going to discuss all of the tools and resources that I recommend to turn you into a fiction-writing machine.

Even though there are a lot of haters out there who can't stand AI, and who pipe up vocally in Facebook groups all the time, I predict that within a few years, every author will be using AI for a least one of the many steps in the writing process.

This is mostly due to the fact that AI is becoming more and more commonplace, especially now that Microsoft, Facebook, Apple and Google are integrating AI with practically all of their devices and software.

As AI becomes a basic, integrated part of all the tools that authors use, it's only a matter of time before they are normalized, and everyone is using them one way or another.

But with that in mind, there are still select groups of people whom I think will benefit the most from using AI. Here is a brief list of who you might be, and why you might be here:

You Should Use AI If...

- **You're just curious:** Even if you don't struggle with

writing, AI can be an engaging experiment. Seeing what an AI can create might spark new ideas or open up creative possibilities you hadn't considered before.

- **You're neurodivergent:** Conditions like ADHD, dyslexia, or being on the autism spectrum often make it very difficult to write in a traditional, structured way. AI tools can provide alternative paths to putting your ideas on paper that are less rigid and taxing.

- **You want to start a publishing company:** Producing a large volume of books to publish under your brand requires immense time and effort. AI allows you to quickly generate quality books so you can get your publishing business up and running at scale.

- **You're burnt out:** Writing can easily become a drain when you're feeling uninspired. AI has innovative techniques to reinvigorate passion projects and provide fresh creative directions. It also reduces the mental strain of writing everything from scratch.

- **You have too many books you want to write:** Even for prolific writers, there are only so many hours in the day. AI enables you to draft and develop multiple book ideas simultaneously. You can get more of the stories in your head created without sacrificing your personal time.

- **You have writer's block:** Staring at a blank page unable to write is incredibly frustrating. AI is uniquely equipped to break through blocks by sparking new directions when you feel stuck. It provides an abstract perspective.

- **You need a brainstorming partner:** Bouncing ideas off another human can get your creative juices flowing. AI provides that same type of sounding board for organizing thoughts and exploring concepts from new angles you might not have considered.

- **You need to improve your writing:** AI can analyze your writing style and point out specific areas for growth and provide concrete examples for how to improve. A human editor provides an indispensable human perspective, while AI provides data-driven recommendations.

- **You want to save time:** Writing something from scratch takes considerable time and effort. With AI you can generate quality content in a fraction of the time once spent on writing. This frees up time for other important tasks.

- **You have a disability:** Physical conditions that limit dexterity or mobility don't have to stop someone from writing with the assistance of AI tools, especially when combined with voice dictation and auto-generating text.

- **You have a language barrier:** For non-native speakers, AI can help translate ideas into coherent writing in their target language. It can also point out errors and suggest corrections to polish writing.

- **Or you have *any* pain point:** Writing is a multi-step process, and most authors don't enjoy at least one of those steps. For me, it's the actual writing. I LOVE the outlining and story-planning stages. And I enjoy the final process of cleaning up the drafts and getting a book ready for publication. But the first draft is a slog. Everyone has different challenges, and AI likely has some application to help alleviate that pain point in one way or another. Get creative with solutions.

And even if you're not planning on letting AI do the writing for you (which it can), it has always been my intention with all of the information I put out to actually turn YOU into a better writer, not because the AI is doing the work for you, but because you use it. A lot of the principles I teach in this book are principles that can be applied with or without AI.

And in the next chapter, I'll briefly discuss why using AI can actually make you a better writer, and help you be *more* creative, not less.

Glossary of Terms

One final bit of housekeeping. Here are a few terms I use throughout the book, and what they mean:

Artificial Intelligence (AI): The use of the term "AI" for generative tools like ChatGPT or AI art generators like Midjourney, is actually a mis-nomer. These tools aren't actually intelligent. Instead, they are using Machine Learning (ML) which allows them to imitate human behavior that they've been trained on, sometimes very convincingly. These tools are also "generative" which is actually a sub-discipline of machine learning. However, given the wide-spread use of the term, I will be using "AI" as a way to refer to these generative tools.

Large Language Model (LLM): Large Language Models are AI models, like GPT-4, trained on extensive text data to generate contextually accurate, human-like text. They use self-attention mechanisms to excel in tasks involving natural language understanding and generation.

Prompt: In the context of AI and specifically language models, a prompt is the input that you give to the model to initiate an output. It's like a starting point or a trigger for the AI to generate text.

Tokens: In natural language processing, a token is a single unit of language that the computer can understand and process. This could be a word, a character, a part of a word (like a sub-word or a phrase), or even a sentence, depending on how tokenization is performed in the specific model. Generally speaking, 1000 tokens is equivalent to (roughly) 750 words.

Natural Language Processing (NLP): A field of AI that focuses on the interaction between computers and humans through natural language. Basically, this is the behind-the-scenes processing that allows the AI to understand what you want, and deliver results.

Part I

AI Foundations

Myth HQ, LLC

3

AI WILL MAKE YOU A BETTER WRITER

The most frequent criticism I get from well-intentioned yet misinformed authors is that using AI makes you lazy. That somehow, by utilizing this incredible technology, you're taking the easy way out and not doing the work required to be an author.

Nothing could be further from the truth.

In reality, I've discovered that writing with AI actually makes you a better writer. It forces you to gain a deeper understanding of story structure, character development, pacing, and all the other intricacies that go into crafting a compelling book.

To properly leverage these tools, you need a solid grasp of the fundamentals. You have to comprehend what makes a good story work and understand the lingo and applications in order to write well with AI. This is exactly the type of practical knowledge we will be covering throughout this book - everything you need to know to become a proficient AI-assisted author.

I've begun to see it happen with authors in my YouTube community. They start out having no clue what goes into writing a book. But by experimenting with AI tools and learning how to guide them, those core storytelling skills develop incredibly quickly.

Let's be clear: writing with AI is still an act of storytelling. The medium for getting the words onto the page is simply different. And it's opening up the craft to those who previously struggled while making experienced authors even better. Once you embrace it, you'll find that human creativity combined with AI is an unstoppable combination.

Here are a few reasons why AI makes you a better writer:

AI Lets You Study Stories in Your Genre

One of the best ways to improve as a writer is to voraciously read books in your genre. Studying how the masters craft stories, develop characters, and utilize literary devices in your niche is invaluable.

But who has time to read for 8 hours a day? This is where AI comes in.

Most AI models, while not perfect and well-read in a lot of modern literature, has a solid understanding of what you are likely to find in a genre. A few prompts let you discover what the major tropes are for that genre, the basic story structure used, and more.

Already, I've found this to be much easier than researching a genre myself, especially when it comes to the broad strokes.

AI Gives You More Time for Deliberate Practice

Deliberate practice - slowly improving through repetition - is crucial for growth. But it requires time. Time that is scarce for most writers.

AI massively expands the clock by dramatically cutting the time spent on early drafts. You focus energy into the high-leverage activities like polishing prose and rehearsing scenes aloud.

Because ideally, authors should be spending time in repetitive practice on a single, specific skill at a time. For example, writing the same scene over and over again with different tenses or points of view. Deliberate practice will dramatically increase your skill as a writer, but most writers don't do it, choosing instead to just continue writing their current book.

But with AI, suddenly you find more hours to devote towards purposeful refinement of your craft, one piece at a time. AI gives back time to concentrate on the work required for mastery.

AI Can Analyze Your Work

Receiving objective feedback is golden. And AI delivers feedback without bias.

And while it's not perfect at this (yet), with AI tools, you can upload chapters and have them extensively analyzed. The AI will identify areas for improvement and offer suggestions based on studying commercially successful books.

And beyond finishing a manuscript, AI can assess your overall style, providing insights into strengths, weaknesses, and opportunities for refinement. Imagine having a developmental editor constantly at your side.

If you're committed to bettering your writing, AI provides invaluable data and diagnostics. Combined with human editors, it's like having a personalized instructor for the craft.

AI Removes Decision Fatigue

Mental stamina is finite. And writing drains it fast. Every sentence requires countless micro-decisions that add up and lead to fatigue.

Should you use this word or that? Is this the right metaphor? Does the dialogue sound natural? The questions never stop.

This is why even great writers can only sustain quality output for a few hours per day. Decision exhaustion sets in.

AI changes the math by eliminating many of these lower-level choices that sap precious mental energy.

This clearance of mundane decisions allows you to channel focus towards more important, big picture choices. Your mental bandwidth is reserved for crafting brilliant scenes rather than debating sentence structure (or vice-versa, depending on how you like to write).

AI Can Suggest Ideas and Techniques You Wouldn't Have Thought Of

Humans have biases. Our creativity is constrained by experience and patterns. This can cause inside-the-box thinking.

AI provides an abstract perspective, unconstrained by convention (most of the time). With the right prompt, it can offer left-field suggestions to break out of tropes and inject novelty.

And its breadth of knowledge is unparalleled. AI has digested millions of books and concepts. It can combine ideas in ways you would have never considered.

Tapping this inventive potential expands your repertoire.

The key is knowing how to effectively prompt the AI. Ask the right questions and you have an imagination machine at your fingertips, limited only by your curiosity.

AI Forces You to Learn Specific Frameworks

To direct an AI assistant, you need to speak its language. This requires learning concrete frameworks for things like story structure, character development, prose, etc.

Suddenly, nebulous concepts like "pacing" become tangible things you can encode into an AI prompt to manipulate. You gain clarity through the constraints of communicating instructions.

The prompts you use end up being mini lessons in writing craft. You must articulate exactly what makes compelling characters and clear prose in order to steer the AI.

This incentivizes you to dig into the specific elements that construct great writing. AI won't just magically produce excellence on its own - you have to guide it there with lucid prompts.

In the process, you rapidly develop the vocabulary and models for discussing writing at a granular level. Your knowledge progresses quickly under the pressure of giving an AI usable instructions.

AI Forces Innovation

When photography was invented, some painters decried it, claiming it would be the death of art. In fact, it had the opposite effect.

Freed from the burden of realism, painters innovated wildly - birthing styles like abstract expressionism and neo-impressionism.

AI is having a similar effect on writing. By transforming drafting, it enables authors to push boundaries and experiment more. Suddenly you have the license to try styles too time intensive to justify before.

History shows again and again that when technology offloads rote work, it increases, rather than decreases, human creativity. AI will keep pushing writing to new heights.

Summary:

- AI forces you to learn storytelling fundamentals to use it effectively.

- AI gives you more time for deliberate practice to refine your craft.

- AI can analyze your writing and provide objective feedback.

- AI removes mundane micro-decisions that drain mental bandwidth.

- AI suggests ideas and techniques you may not have considered.

- Using AI requires learning specific writing frameworks.

- The constraints of prompting AI deepens your

knowledge.

- AI enables more experimentation and innovation.

4

THE STORY HACKING METHOD

I remember the first time I read Eragon by Christopher Paolini. I was in my teens and, as a sucker for a good fantasy story, immediately fell in love with the first novel. It had everything I liked:

- A young hero who, as we discover, is the last of a long line of mystical warriors

- A roguish side character

- An old mentor figure who tragically dies mid-way through the story

- The rescue of a beautiful woman who is mysteriously held by the forces of darkness

- A band of rebels

And...wait a minute, I'd heard this story before.

As a matter of fact, it was no wonder I loved Eragon, because it perfectly modeled my favorite story universe of all time (to this day): George Lucas' Star Wars.

And believe it or not, this sort of thing is quite common, especially among bestsellers.

Now, Eragon has received some criticism for being almost TOO derivative of Star Wars. But that criticism ignores the fact that it was written by a teenager (which alone is impressive), that fans (especially younger fans) loved the story, and it launched the career of that teenager into the ranks of full-time authorship, earning him tons of money, leading to a movie deal (which we won't talk about), and essentially ensuring the author a place in publishing for the rest of his life. He's still releasing books, and they are much more well-received, critically, since he has had time to grow as an author.

And I don't care how derivative a story is (as long as it's not infringing on copyright). Results are what matter here, and Christopher Paolini certainly got results.

So what was it about Eragon that resonated with enough people to launch Christopher Paolini's career?

Well, it's impossible to pin-point any one thing, but as I've since come to learn after *extensive* study of bestselling novels, success like this is more predictable than many care to think.

Because bestselling stories have things in common.

And as much as some people try to deny it, almost every good piece of writing can be broken down into component parts, analyzed, and reused for commercial gain.

So in other words, Christopher Paolini, whether consciously or not, mimicked the plot of Star Wars, but with enough of the author's own spin on the story to make it unique. At least, unique enough to be considered original and not the subject of a lawsuit.

Star Wars was not the first either. George Lucas was drawing heavily from multiple sources, including Joseph Campbell's Hero's Journey framework, the films of Akira Kurosawa, and the old serials of his childhood like Flash Gordon and Buck Rodgers. And when you go back and watch those films, serials, and learn of the Hero's Journey, you realize just how closely Lucas was modeling those frameworks.

Point to any bestseller, and I'll bet I can point to a handful of key influences that the author pulled from, or frameworks that are common among bestselling fiction.

The Hero's Journey is perhaps the most well-known framework, used in most bestselling fiction of the last few decades, from Harry Potter to James Cameron's Avatar.

So what does this have to do with AI?

Well, I'll talk later about the importance of frameworks in my F.I.T.S. model. But put simply, frameworks are essential to get the best results out of AI.

And this process of examining fiction-related frameworks and studying them is a process that I call **Story Hacking**.

Story hacking is the process of finding frameworks in bestselling fiction, then modeling those frameworks in your own work. In the context of AI, it can also mean taking those frameworks and using them to craft specific prompts that can be used to improve the quality of AI output.

I came up with this term after studying the business models established by online marketing guru, Russell Brunson. In his books, I learned of a term he had called "Funnel Hacking", which was basically the process of examining the business structures, sales pages, webinars, etc. of successful entrepreneurs, then modeling those frameworks in your own business.

Believe it or not, this is the exact same process that many bestselling authors have used to become bestsellers. They've taken established stories that resonate with audiences, broken them down into their component parts, then modeled those works with their own spin on the story.

Bear in mind that this is perfectly legal. We're not talking about copying or plagiarizing anything. We're *modeling,* and there's a big difference.

I've gone through dozens of courses about writing craft, and read even more books. Almost all of these experts who study fiction for a living agree that there are replicable patterns across all bestselling media.

For instance, David Wolverton, the mentor of Brandon Sanderson, Stephenie Meyer, and many others, mentions that most bestselling stories take people to "another time, and another place."

James Scott Bell talks about his LOCK system, which is a basic framework he's identified in bestselling fiction. (James is a wizard-level Story Hacker)

And of course, there's the Hero's Journey, which has been at the heart of so many bestselling stories for ages.

Story Hacking is the process of identifying those frameworks and then using them in your own work.

When using AI, an essential skill I recommend you develop is this process of Story Hacking. It's not exactly an AI-exclusive kind of skill, but it is an essential *writing* skill, and one AI can help you with.

Because AI thrives on frameworks, the skill of Story Hacking is a must if you want to steer the AI in the direction you want to go. For example, if you use an outline for your novel, you are already using a Story Hacked formula, but you can find many more by studying what others have written, or selecting a story you want to model and breaking it down yourself.

For example, over the last year or so, I've been working on a novel that's part of a "medieval academy" genre. There are only a few bestselling series in this genre, so I bought them, and I've been reading through them and taking notes (scene by scene) of what they are doing, so I can model the frameworks later.

But it's not just outlines. My chapter on Brainstorming, for example, contains prompts that I developed after analyzing frameworks from James Scott Bell and others. These were techniques that these fiction experts had identified as good for brainstorming, and then I simply found a way to fashion them into prompts that work in ChatGPT or Claude.

This is the perfect use of Story Hacking: finding a formula that works, then crafting it into a prompt.

I did the same thing when coming up with my prompts for Story Beats. My original story beats prompt was a lot more generic, like "give me 12 story beats for the following chapter description." But once I learned that every scene has structure, and there are certain benchmarks that should ideally be hit, I was able to craft a prompt that was much better at getting specific results.

I'm sure I'll be able to craft even better prompts as I learn more and story hack other bestsellers.

This is why "Story Hacker Secrets" is the name of this book series. Any subsequent books I write in this series will all be centered around this idea: finding the formulas that work, the tools that authors can use with or without AI.

So with that in mind, I encourage you to become Story Hackers, people who not only use frameworks with AI, but who are actively seeking out more frameworks to use. You'll find them among bestsellers generally, but also maybe you just have a single story that you want to emulate in some way, or a single character you love. Many of the best stories were created with this kind of influence. AI only makes it more fun.

But there is a lot more to working with AI than just gathering your framework. There's a certain collaborative skill that you will need to foster as you practice using these large language models. I'll cover that in the next chapter.

Summary:

- Story hacking involves analyzing successful stories to identify common frameworks and patterns. These can then be modeled in your own writing.

- Many bestselling stories follow similar narrative structures like the Hero's Journey. Identifying these shared elements can help craft more resonant stories.

- Studying the techniques of successful authors reveals useful storytelling tools. These can be adapted into writing prompts.

- Frameworks are essential for getting good results from AI. Prompts based on proven storytelling formulas will produce higher quality AI output.

- "Story Hacker" means not just using frameworks with AI, but actively seeking more tools and narrative patterns to incorporate. This ongoing research elevates writing skills.

5

THE BEST AI TOOLS FOR FICTION

When you Google the "Best AI Tool for Fiction" a lot of results will come up of people who clearly don't know what they're talking about. You end up with a long list of generic AI tools, and it's clear that the author never wrote a fiction book in their life.

Well, I have.

And this was partly what inspired me to start my YouTube channel in the first place. When I got started, no one (and I mean that) was making YouTube videos about writing fiction with AI that had experience as a real fiction writer.

And after writing 14 books the traditional way, as well as three years of experience at Kindlepreneur teaching authors about craft, I thought I had a decent handle on how to write. So before we get deeper into this book, I'd like to outline the best tools for writing fiction.

Unlike nonfiction AI writing, there are only a few good options, so this will not be a lengthy list.

Each has their own pros and cons, which I'll give here. I'll also present my favorite tool for writing fiction.

But First: Models vs Tools

Before I start listing specific AI tools, it's important to understand the difference between different AI *models* and AI *tools*.

AI Models are the underlying Large Language Model (LLM) that most of the tools use. Each model is unique and usually has certain tasks that it is better at than others. Well-known models (as of this writing) include GPT-4o, Claude 3 Opus, Claude 3.5 Sonnet, Mistral Large, Llama 3 70B, etc.

AI Tools are pieces of software that *use* AI models in an integrated way. They are like a wrapper that developers put around the AI models to harness their power in a specific way. Some of them are exclusive to a single company's models (like ChatGPT), but others incorporate dozens of models from multiple companies.

I'm not going to list my favorite models here, because they change so frequently. I will only mention that the Claude family of models are usually my favorite, and have been since I first started using them, even though more recent models are far more advanced than the early ones. However, that could easily change in the future as new models are released.

The Best AI Writing Tools for Fiction

The following are, I believe, the best tools for fiction.

1. Novelcrafter

2. Claude Pro

3. The OpenAI Playground

4. Sudowrite

Let's go through these one by one.

1. Novelcrafter

Cost: $4/month for Scribe (no AI), $8/month for Hobbyist, $14/month for Artisan, $20/month for Specialist. I recommend the $14/month Artisan tier.

Pros:

- Extreme flexibility

- Allows access to fine-tuned models

- Low cost

- Lots of features

- Built with fiction writers in mind

- Seemless integration of AI

- No content restrictions

Cons:

- Slight learning curve

- AI tokens are pay as you go

Novelcrafter is my top choice for a writing tool for fiction authors that uses AI.

Novelcrafter came onto the scene in late 2023 and took the AI writing world by storm. Its innovative Codex and Prompting features, not to mention the fact that you could use *any* AI model inside of it, was a huge deal.

Before Novelcrafter, the big kid on the block was Sudowrite, but Novelcrafter immediately had some major advantages over Sudowrite. First, it allowed you to have unlimited AI words, as long as you were willing to pay for them, and the cost was about as cheap as it's possible to be. Sudowrite, on the other hand, had fixed number of words that you get with each plan, and to get more costs a lot more than you get with Novelcrafter. Plus, depending on the plan in Sudowrite, you might not get to keep the words if you don't use them that month.

Novelcrafter, on the other hand, was extremely flexible, allowing authors to connect to an OpenRouter account for all their AI model needs (way more models than any other platform). Plus, this also allows you to access fine-tuned models that you may have created in the OpenAI Playground, and integrate them into Novelcrafter, something you can't do with Sudowrite. That's why the base cost of Novelcrafter is so cheap, because it doesn't include AI words. Now this often *appears* as a drawback for some authors, the fact that you have to pay extra for the AI words that you use. But for most people, you won't actually be spending more on the AI words than you would if you were using Sudowrite or ChatGPT Plus.

While I could go deep on all of the features that Novelcrafter provides, suffice it to say that it has everything I could possibly want as an author using AI. You can integrate basically any LLM for whatever occasion, and Novelcrafter's interface makes it easy to interact with the LLMs in a way built specifically for fiction writers.

Also, it can also do nonfiction, if you're into that.

The Bottom Line: While requiring a slight learning curve, Novelcrafter is by far the best AI writing tool because it is designed very specifically with authors in mind, and with a clear understanding of the challenges that AI authors need to overcome.

You can find it at this link: https://nerdynovelist.com/go/novelcrafter

2. Claude

Cost: $20 for Pro

Pros:

- Has 200K tokens, meaning it has a massive memory

- Built with safety and alignment in mind

- The best LLMs at crafting realistic prose

Cons:

- Limited in certain parameters and functionalities from being a chatbot

Claude is an AI chatbot from Anthropic that aims to provide useful, ethical conversation. Anthropic is known for trying its best to take a more ethical, cautious approach.

And I don't know what it is about their language models, but Claude is absolutely fantastic at writing prose. Way better than ChatGPT, no question.

PLUS, it has a very large token limit, meaning you can fit an entire book in there, and it will remember what happened. This is helpful for creating a story bible, or feeding it all of the information that you want it to remember during your chat.

The Claude family of models are many by this point, and more will continue to come out, but almost all of them have proven to have better and more human-sounding prose. Plus I find it to be just as good as the GPT models for writing tasks like outlining, brainstorming, researching, and more.

Claude Pro is specifically a $20/month subscription that gives you increased access to the Claude models, and access to a few other important features like Projects, which I actually genuinely find useful.

The only major downside of Claude Pro is that it's a chatbot, which means that you don't have the same fine-tuned control that you might have in a program like Novelcrafter, which allows you to adjust more advanced sliders for each of the models, like Temperature and Top P. However, I find having a chatbot like this is useful, and it's entirely possible to write a whole book with just a chatbot (I did it in a series of livestreams in November of 2023). If you have good prompts, you can do it.

I, however, use it primarily for brainstorming and more conversational-like chats, rather than for actually writing parts of the book. For that, I use Novelcrafter.

The Bottom Line: For the best prose and most creativity, Claude is definitely a tool you should look at.

You can find it at this link: https://nerdynovelist.com/go/claude

3. OpenAI Playground

Cost: Varies based on the model. Pay as you go.

Pros:

- Everything ChatGPT provides

- Extreme flexibility

- Inexpensive

- Can edit past responses

Cons:

- Pay as you go

OpenAI Playground is basically the same as ChatGPT Plus, but with a few differences.

And the Playground actually has one advantage over ChatGPT: you can edit past responses. So if it writes something, then I go through and edit that response, it will remember my edited version and not the response it gave (although it can only remember so much before you have to start deleting past responses).

The big downside here is that the Playground is pay as you go. It's relatively inexpensive, especially for older models, but once again I find this limits what I want to do with it. With ChatGPT I can just keep iterating and trying new things, which I don't want to do with Playground.

Additionally, you have to pay for any words you want it to remember. So even though you can edit the past responses, you'll be paying for any words you leave in the window, as it requires processing power to analyze those words.

If you don't use AI very often, this isn't a huge issue. It will still be very affordable. But if you use AI a lot in your writing, you may find it more economical to use ChatGPT or Claude.

The Bottom Line: OpenAI's Playground is the most freeing way to use ChatGPT's features, but without actually having to subscribe to ChatGPT. Plus, even though it's pay as you go, the chances that you'll actually exceed the $20/month price tag of ChatGPT is relatively low.

You can find it at this link: https://nerdynovelist.com/go/openaiplayground

4. Sudowrite

Cost: $19/month for 225K credits, $29/month for 1M credits, $59/month for 2M credits. I recommend the $29/month tier.

Pros:

- Lots of features

- Simple design

- Great for authors who don't want to be prompt engineers

- Built with fiction writers in mind

Cons:

- No way to access models they don't specifically include

- No way to access fine-tuned models

- Some features have poor design

- The most expensive on this list

In the realm of AI and writing tools, Sudowrite was one of the first to capture the attention of fiction writers. It was, and continues to be, one of the most powerful programs out there.

Sudowrite's extensive features can be categorized into writing tools, revision tools, brainstorming tools, and others. Writing tools like First Draft, Guided and Auto Write, Tone Shift, and Expand help in the initial stages of crafting a manuscript. Revision tools such as Rewrite and Describe aid in polishing the manuscript.

It does a lot of what Novelcrafter does, and the two are actually quite similar. In fact, most authors would probably be fine with one over the other.

However, Sudowrite has some downsides, including a pricing structure that I don't care for. For example, the $29/month tier gives you 1,000,000 credits per month, which can translate to a variety of word counts, depending on which models you are using. If you don't use those credits words, you lose them (unless you're on the highest $59/month plan), but it's actually possible to burn through those words extremely fast, unlike ChatGPT or Claude, where you have an unlimited amount of text generation for what you pay for.

Additionally, because Sudowrite is providing the AI words for you, rather than integrating a third-party AI provider like OpenRouter (as Novelcrafter does), this means that you are limited in the models you can select. This is especially an issue if you have created fine-tuned models in OpenAI's platform, which are not useable at all inside of Sudowrite.

But that said, Sudowrite is probably the easiest to navigate and to use AI if you're not a prompt engineer. If you find prompting and using AI to be overwhelming, then Sudowrite might actually be the best option for you, because it's very user friendly.

The Bottom Line: For tools that are specifically built for fiction, Sudowrite may be a good options, especially if you're looking for user-friendliness.

You can find it at this link: https://nerdynovelist.com/go/sudowrite

Verdict: Which Should You Use?

For most authors, I usually recommend a combination of Novelcrafter with at least one chatbot, of which Claude Pro is my favorite. ChatGPT or Gemini will work as well, though.

However, if you could only have one platform, I would recommend Novelcrafter, as you can get chatbot-like capabilities inside of Novelcrafter as long as you have the Artisan plan.

Honorable Mentions:

You'll notice a few tools that you may have heard of but are not included on this list. Here are a few:

- **ChatGPT:** While a useful tool, I find it doesn't provide that much value to warrant the paid Plus account. You can get everything you need from the OpenAI Playground mentioned above, and most likely without the same expense.

- **Gemini:** Google's own chatbot is also very powerful, and many authors find it excels at specific tasks, like brainstorming. However, between it, ChatGPT, and Claude, I prefer Claude.

- **Poe:** There's a website called Poe that costs the same as ChatGPT Plus, Claude Pro, or Gemini Advanced. The advantage that Poe has is that it contains all of those models, so if you want the best of all worlds, Poe might be a good option. However, I've found Poe to be somewhat limited in the responses that it gives and the usage output. Personally I prefer having the paid version of Claude Pro, then only using the free versions of ChatGPT and Gemini if/when I need them.

- **OpenRouter:** This is similar to Poe, but instead of a subscription it's pay as you go. You will likely need an OpenRouter account if you plan to use Novelcrafter, because you can then integrate the two. It's a powerful program but lacking in terms of interface, which is what Novelcrafter excels at.

- **Jasper:** This is one of the more well-known AI tools out there, but it's more geared for nonfiction, and I've found that it offers little that I can't get from a chatbot alone, or from tools like Novelcrafter. It definitely SHOULD NOT be used for fiction writing.

In this book, I'll be referring to all of these tools, depending on which one makes sense for which step of the process. But most of the principles I teach in this book are designed to work with all of them, especially the chatbots like ChatGPT and Claude.

And understanding how to use those tools will make it much easier to use tools like Novelcrafter or Sudowrite, which is built on the backs of various LLMs.

Whew! Now we've got all of the preamble out of the way, it's time to buckle down and start actually learning all this "prompt engineering" stuff. Let's get into it!

Summary:

- AI models are the underlying language processing engines (like GPT-4 or Claude), while AI tools are software applications that integrate these models to provide specific functionalities for users.

- My top recommended AI writing tools for fiction are:

    a. Novelcrafter ($14/month Artisan tier recommended)

    b. Claude Pro ($20/month)

    c. OpenAI Playground (pay-as-you-go)

    d. Sudowrite ($29/month tier recommended)

- Each tool has its pros, cons, costs, and unique features, with Novelcrafter being my top choice for its flexibility and fiction-specific design.

- I recommend using a combination of Novelcrafter and a chatbot like Claude Pro for most writers, but the techniques taught in this book can apply to multiple tools

6

THE F.I.T.S. FRAMEWORK

Frameworks. You're going to hear me talk a lot about frameworks. They are, without a doubt, the single, most important concept to understand, not just for working with AI, but for producing good fiction.

I was first introduced to the immense power of frameworks when I read some of Russell Brunson's books, specifically DotCom Secrets and Expert Secrets. He emphasizes how frameworks exist everywhere if you just know how to look for them.

Plus, his books are full of frameworks, strategies and steps that make online business seem simple.

Side note: if you're interested in creating an online business, I cannot recommend Russell's books more. You can get DotCom Secrets (which is where I recommend you start) for free with shipping by visiting this link: https://nerdynovelist.com/go/dotcomsecrets

All this talk of frameworks really got me thinking about how Russell's observations were true in the world of fiction writing, especially when analyzing bestsellers. There are clearly identifiable patterns and frameworks underlying most successful stories (I'll talk more about this in the next chapter).

And I realized the same is true when it comes to creating effective AI prompts. Certain frameworks lend themselves to producing coherent, high-quality output from AI.

Intrigued by these ideas, I set out to find the frameworks for fiction writing and AI prompting. I watched hundreds of hours of YouTube tutorials, took online courses, and pored through writing books. Slowly, some recurring patterns began to emerge.

After refining these key concepts down to their core essence, I eventually arrived at what I call the F.I.T.S Framework. This simple yet robust model encapsulates the key elements of strong AI prompting in an easy-to-grasp acronym.

While many writers utilize similar concepts intuitively, the F.I.T.S Framework explains them clearly.

So without further ado, let me introduce you to this game changing framework.

F.I.T.S. stands for **Framework**, **Identity**, **Task**, and **Style**.

These four elements apply to 99% of the prompts you will use, especially if you write fiction.

Let's walk through each section one-by-one...

1. Framework

Out of the entire F.I.T.S. process, nothing is more crucial than establishing a clear framework. This is the backbone that brings coherence and direction to your AI assistant. Without it, you can prompt all day long, but your results will be aimless ramblings.

Let's unpack why a defined framework is so key when leveraging AI chatbots:

Without the use of a framework, an AI chatbot will almost always default to highly generalized, over-used cliches and boring ideas.

There's a common saying, first coined (as near as I can tell) by game designer, Mark Rosewater, that says "restrictions breed creativity."

This is as true (if not more so) for AI as it is for humans.

By providing an AI with a specific framework for the story you want to create, you give it guard rails to follow. Instead of meandering aimlessly with its boundless knowledge, it now has a path to funnel it down productively.

Just think about a framework as the boundaries within which you want the AI to operate and generate ideas. These could include a detailed outline, a set of defined characters, examples of the type of content that you want, etc. The more details you provide, the more targeted the output will be.

For example, story structures like the Hero's Journey, Save the Cat, or Story Circle are the perfect examples of frameworks, though only for outlining.

But the applications go far beyond just story outlines. Frameworks can be created for any part of the writing process where you want to constrain the AI within optimized creative boundaries.

Want to brainstorm dynamic character profiles? Create a character sheet framework. Need a description-rich setting? Build a framework that has the AI focus solely on that.

The key is specificity. When prompting an AI assistant, you always want to start broad and then get progressively more detailed with the framework. Broad frameworks lead to broad outputs. Detailed frameworks give you polished results.

If you can't tell, I'm a little obsessed with frameworks, and I'm pretty sure that any other books I choose to write about storytelling, will just be collections of frameworks, lol.

But seriously, it's an important concept. That's why it occupies the crucial first step in the F.I.T.S. method. Get this piece right, and everything else falls nicely into place.

2. Identity

The I in F.I.T.S stands for Identity. This step involves giving your AI assistant a particular persona to inhabit while generating content for you.

This is actually one of the biggest commonalities I found while studying up on AI prompting. Everyone is using this method, because it works.

Establishing a clear identity produces way more targeted results than just asking an AI to write generally. It allows you to shape the knowledge and voice of the AI however you desire by creating a fictional identity for it to assume.

For instance, if you're researching a historical fiction set in medieval France, you would prompt the AI to adopt the identity of a historian with over 30 years of experience re-searching medieval European culture.

This immediately tunes the output to your needs.

Possible identities are infinite, bounded only by your imagination. Here are just a few examples:

- A bestselling thriller author with 20 years experience and 50 published books.

- A world class creative writing professor at Harvard.

- A fantasy fiction super fan who has read 500+ novels in the genre.

- A poet with a melancholy style and focus on nature themes.

- A casual blogger writing a humorous travel journal.

And you can assign multiple identities tailored to different parts of the project. Swap easily between a historian identity when researching and a commercial fiction writer identity when drafting.

One quick note on dialing in the perfect identity - I've found it makes a big difference when establishing expertise to specify years of experience. An identity framed as a seasoned 20-year veteran professional will generate very different content than framing it as an unpaid intern just getting their feet wet.

3. Task

If Framework and Identity cover the broader steering of the AI to keep it on track, Task represents the specific job you want it to complete in the moment. This is where you directly state the content you want generated.

For example:

- Write a short fantasy story about a knight rescuing a dragon.

- Describe a magical forest in vivid sensory detail.

- Analyze the themes and symbolism in the first chapter of my novel.

The Task is typically a simple, straightforward request. You've set up the boundaries and persona in the previous steps, now you directly tell the AI what content you want created within those confines.

I like to think of Task statements being similar to prompts you would give a human personal assistant. Concise, action-oriented requests like:

- Please write a 300 word blog post about AI content creation.

- Can you expand these notes into a compelling scene?

- I need help fleshing out character profiles based on these outlines.

Once you've established the framing clearly, the Task allows you to make focused content requests without having to reiterate all the context each time.

Keep it simple and direct here. Short, clearly defined assignments keep the AI on track and signal exactly what output you want produced.

Of the elements of F.I.T.S., this step requires the least creative work on your end. But well-defined Tasks are crucial to keeping your AI assistant productive and generating content tailored specifically to your needs.

4. Style

The final piece of the F.I.T.S. puzzle is Style. This step is about providing instructions to the AI on the particular tone, diction, and flair you want present in the generated content.

While Framework, Identity, and Task handle the broader shaping of the output, Style focuses entirely on stylistic elements like:

- Tone - Serious, humorous, romantic, mysterious, etc.

- Diction - Simple/complex word choices and phrasing

- Point of view - First person, third person, etc.

- Verbosity - Long winded or terse and to the point

- Literary techniques - Metaphors, alliteration, hyperbole, etc.

Specifying a clear Style aligns the AI's output more closely with your unique writer's voice. Without guidance, AI writing can tend towards generic and formulaic. The Style step gives you granular control to craft a customized voice.

For example, you can make the Style:

- Lean heavily on figurative language like metaphors to convey emotions.

- Use shorter, choppier sentence structure reminiscent of hard-boiled detective stories.

- Employ a liberal sprinkling of adjectives and adverbs when describing scenes.

- Adopt a breezy, conversational first-person narration.

Ideally, provide the AI with some samples of your own writing to analyze and emulate. This "tuning" of the Style to match your natural voice is a fun process. It's also the process that requires the most experimentation.

Now Style guidance is optional. It's not necessary for things like brainstorming or outlining, where voice doesn't matter. But for drafting quality prose, it takes the output to the next level.

While Framework, Identity, and Task form the key foundational pieces; Style is the icing on top. It's the final step for elevating technically sound writing into truly artful prose infused with your one-of-a-kind writer's touch.

Examples of a Good F.I.T.S. Prompt

By now, you already know enough to be dangerous. And it'll start to annoy you (sorry, not sorry) when you see others entering horribly simple prompts and then bemoaning the state of AI when they don't get good results.

AI is 100% capable of producing amazing output. But you have to prompt it right, and using F.I.T.S is the first step to doing so.

But what are some examples of what this looks like in practice? Well, there are infinite possibilities, but here are some examples of a simple F.I.T.S. prompt, as well as a more complicated one.

Simple F.I.T.S. Prompt:

You are an advanced science fiction romance author, with 20 years experience and you've written 50 books [IDENTITY] Write me an outline for a science fiction beach romance [TASK] using the Hero's Journey model [FRAMEWORK] in the structural style of a Jules Verne novel [STYLE].

Advanced F.I.T.S. Prompt:

You are an experienced and prolific fantasy fiction author who has published over 30 bestselling novels and has 40 years of experience. Your stories are known for vivid worldbuilding and morally complex characters. You have a PhD in mythology and Jungian psychology, which informs your symbolic writing style. [IDENTITY]

I'd like you to write 500 words of a scene, using the following story summary: [TASK]

Lyra and Elara sit together in the mess hall, discussing their day and sharing a meal. We get a description of the mess hall and a little bit of information about Brightsoul Academy. Lyra is incredibly nervous, and is hardly eating. Elara eventually has to ask why. The opening line should be about how Lyra is nervous because this will be the day that she raise the dead for the first time. Lyra hesitantly brings up her concerns about raising the dead. She's worried that she might not succeed, and mentions her friend, Arin, who had previously left the academy because she found raising the dead and forcing them to be slaves to be immoral. Lyra speculates if Arin was right, and if Lyra isn't making a horrible mistake by becoming a necromancer. [FRAMEWORK]

Do it in first person past point of view of Lyra. Be sure to show don't tell, and use deep point of view. Have realistic dialogue, stronger verbs, lots of conflict, drama, and description. Avoid mushy descriptions and dialogue. [STYLE]

As you can see, these prompts can get quite lengthy, so you might be wondering: is this really a productivity assistant? It looks like some of the prompts are just as long as the outputs they're designed to create.

Well, the good news is that, quite often, these prompts can be reused. You just swap out the right part, and go again. So the more experience you get, and the more prompts you collect (and yes, it starts to feel like a collection), the faster you will become. Additionally, many tools like Novelcrafter will facilitate the placement of a lot of the different component parts of your prompt.

But a good prompt is just the beginning. You have to have the right structures first, otherwise your fiction will be generic and boring. So what can we do to get the best kind of output from AI? That's what I'll cover in the next chapter.

Summary:

- F.I.T.S. stands for Framework, Identity, Task, and Style

- Framework provides the boundaries and context for the AI.

- Identity gives the AI a persona to inhabit while generating content.

- Task is a direct request for what content you want

created.

- Style shapes the tone, diction, and flair of the output.

- Prompts can be reused and expanded over time.

7

KEY SKILL: COLLABORATION

Whenever I'm planning out the stories in a book, or I'm stuck in some way, I used to call my mom. To be clear, my mom knows *nothing* about writing books. Nothing at all. But there was something about vocalizing my thoughts out loud that never failed to crystallize them. I would describe the premise, the characters, and the various plot threads I envisioned weaving together. It helped me bring the story more into focus. And honestly, my mom wasn't doing more than listening.

Now married, it's my wife who hears my ramblings about imaginary people and places. She provides a listening ear and, when needed, a gentle push in the right direction.

I've even had engaging back-and-forths with God, believe it or not. On long, quiet walks, I will talk out loud about my works in progress. Even though He surely has bigger things to worry about than my fiction, I like to imagine He cares about my interests. I'll then try to listen as He talks back to me, because I believe He cares about what I'm working on.

Now with AI, those same creative conversations occur, except rather than speaking aloud, they transpire through text prompts and responses. But the collaborative effect is much the same. The AI becomes a knowledgeable partner, helping to refine fuzzy notions and illuminate unseen connections.

When using AI for fiction writing, <u>there is no more important skill than the iterative and collaborative process of conversing with the AI.</u>

So often we envision prompt engineering as one-and-done interactions - type a prompt, get some output, and move on. But the magic happens through an evolving collaboration, not isolated transactions.

If you want to succeed at writing with AI, you must learn to progressively build on the initial responses the AI generates. Each output becomes a springboard for the next exchange.

This chapter covers proven techniques for engaging in truly synergistic collaboration with AI writing assistants. The key is viewing them not merely as convenient tools, but as creative partners. When treated as such, you'll be amazed at the storytelling possibilities that open up through the iterative process.

So let's look at a few techniques.

1. Treat the AI Like a Writing Partner

When I first started using AI assistants for fiction writing, I viewed them like convenient tools - magical keyboards that could churn out paragraphs on command. I'd bark an order, text would appear, and I'd move on to the next task.

It didn't take long for me to realize this perspective was hugely limiting. The outputs were often rambling and incoherent.

If you can shift to view the AI as a collaborative writing partner, not an on-demand text generator, and start treating it like a junior writing intern, the results will improve dramatically.

Remember that an AI has no true creative agenda. You can explore options and then effortlessly redirect it without causing offense. The technology becomes an extension of your imagination.

Approaching AI writing as a collaboration provides a positive feedback loop. Treat it like a colleague, not a computer, and watch your partnership boom.

2. Ask Follow-Up Questions

This is the easiest way to learn how to collaborate with AI, simply start asking it follow-up questions, instead of taking what it says verbatim. Doing so actually causes it to refine the data set it's using, opening up new pathways to explore, which color the otherwise generic tone/knowledge that AI usually gives you to start.

It's one of the best ways to get it to be less generic.

3. Give Light Edits and Corrections

While AI assistants can generate coherent content, their skills are far from perfect. So I will often edit what it gives me, then feed that back into the AI so it knows the style I'm going for, and can then refine its output closer to what I'm looking for as I go.

(Note: I've been doing it a lot for this chapter.)

Giving edits to AI writing is a little like pruning a bush into an aesthetically pleasing shape. Once the AI knows the shape you're going for, it's much better at pruning the next bush.

This fine-tuning progressively trains the AI on your personal writing style. Over time, you mold it into a customized writing companion.

4. Request Alternate Versions

An easy way to improve results is simply asking the AI to generate a handful of different versions for a given request.

For example, instead of accepting the first description of a character, I'll say:

"Can I get 5 different possible descriptions of the hero's physical appearance?"

Or when asking for plot developments:

"Provide me with 10 potential plot twists that could upend the trajectory of the story."

Out of several options, there is usually one that stands out from the pack. I'll choose that strongest response and then have the AI continue building off of it.

This technique of culling the most promising content strand works for scenes, settings, dialogue - pretty much any element.

It leverages the AI's tendency for randomness to provide variational fodder. You pick the winners and then iterate upon them.

The key is regularly asking for different versions to keep possibilities multiplying. Don't just accept the machine's first output.

5. Have it Ask You Questions

One of my favorite collaborative techniques is prompting the AI to act as an inquisitive tutor and asking *me* the questions, for a change.

For example, here is a prompt I used in a video:

"Pretend you are an expert economist with 30 years of experience and an extensive knowledge of economic books and papers. I'd like to create a story based around the concept of a true, working utopia, and you are going to help me figure this out. Be sure to ask questions before you answer, in order to probe deeper."

And this was the response it gave me:

That sounds like an exciting project, and I'd be delighted to assist. Before we proceed, it's important to clarify certain aspects to ensure we're on the same page. A "utopia" can mean different things to different people. Here are some questions that will help me tailor my responses to your specific needs:

What is your definition of a "utopia"? Are we considering a society that is ideal in all aspects such as economic, social, political, and environmental? Or are we focusing primarily on the economic aspect?

What kind of economic system does this utopia operate under? Capitalist, socialist, mixed economy, or something entirely new?

What are the critical aspects of this utopia's economic success? Are we looking at things like wealth equality, high standard of living, robust growth, environmental sustainability, or all of these and more?

How does this utopia deal with classic economic problems such as scarcity, opportunity cost, and economic decision making?

Does this utopia have interactions with other non-utopian societies or is it completely isolated?

What is the technological level of this society? High-tech, low-tech, or somewhere in between?

How does this utopia handle human desires and needs? Is it based on complete satisfaction, or is there a different mechanism in place to manage these?

Once we have a more detailed outline of your utopian vision, we can start crafting the story.

I was able to answer the questions, and it probed even deeper, making this a rather rich and interesting thought experiment, one that went far deeper than I would have done by just asking the AI questions, or brainstorming on my own.

This role reversal provides an entirely new perspective. The AI's outside eye pinpoints gaps I'm too close to see. It also accesses a diverse repertoire of coaching frameworks to systematically analyze my story's strengths and weaknesses.

I'd say try it if you're stuck.

Summary:

- Treat the AI like a writing colleague, not just a tool.

- Ask follow-up questions to refine responses.

- Provide light edits for the AI to learn your style.

- Request multiple alternate versions and pick the best.

- Have the AI reverse roles and ask you questions.

- Iterative collaboration unlocks the AI's potential more than one-off prompts.

Part II

The Fractal Method

Myth HQ, LLC

8

The Fractal Method

I t was December of 2022, ChatGPT had just come out, and everyone was blown away by it. I was no exception. I was spending hours testing its limits, and seeing if it could even be used to write fiction.

But try as I might, I just couldn't get it to work.

I would ask it to write a specific story, and it would provide something that would have worked for a surface-level storybook, but not for an in-depth novel where we need things like deep point of view, showing instead of telling, and more. I wasn't sure what to do.

At that time, there were no courses to take, nothing to guide me, other than to watch a few YouTube videos from other people like me who were still experimenting with the language model.

And that's where I found the answer.

I wasn't even sure who it was who finally explained it to me, and it wasn't even about fiction at the time, it was about writing a blog post.

In the video, the YouTuber talked about how he progressed from an outline, to a more detailed outline, and finally to the finished result. He would prompt ChatGPT to generate an outline, then he would move into the first part of that outline, and would have it create a bulleted list of things to talk about within that section. It was a much more detailed outline than I would have done myself (knowing what I did then).

But the next part was what blew me away. Now that he had a detailed outline, he was able to generate much better prose than before, prose that went far more in-depth, and that felt closer to the way a human would write about that topic.

I knew I had to test this out with fiction.

Now, at this time, I was working with the GPT-3.5 language model, so the results weren't as stellar as I can get today. But when I moved through this process of taking a story by the outline first, then moving into a more detailed outline, and then from there moving into the finished prose, I got much better results.

My mind was blown! It was the first time I really realized that AI was going places that could help me get over burnout and expand my business.

I've since seen this technique used hundreds of times by different authors, for fiction and nonfiction. But I finally decided to take all of these examples and refine them into a suitable framework for authors to follow.

And that's how the Fractal Technique was born (although I'd like to quickly give a shout out to Elizabeth Ann West for helping me come up with the name).

The Fractal Technique allows authors to rapidly generate ideas, outlines, and draft material. It takes inspiration from traditional outlining methods, but optimizes them to tap into AI's unique capabilities.

What is a Fractal?

Before diving into the specifics, it's helpful to understand what a fractal is. Fractals are infinitely complex patterns that exhibit similar details at every scale. They are generated mathematically and contain endless nuances the deeper you look.

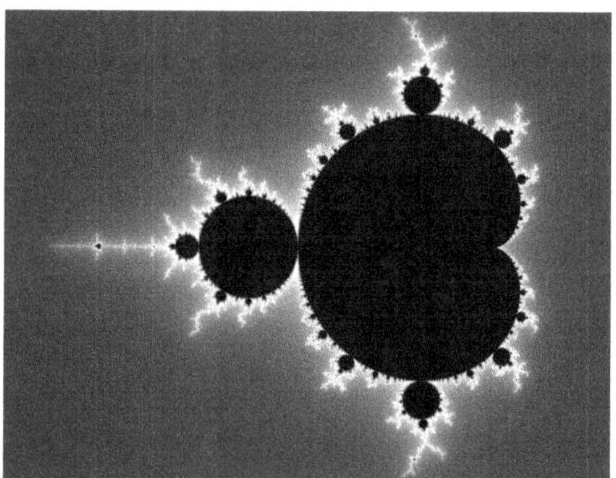

A classic example is the Mandelbrot set. As you zoom in on the pattern, more and more intricate details emerge. No matter how far you magnify the image, there are always finer fractal shapes to discover.

This concept is the foundation of the Fractal Technique. The idea is to start with a high-level concept and then drill down into more detail, creating a rich, detailed narrative.

Step 1: Generate the Loglines

The first step in the Fractal Technique is to generate high-concept pitches or loglines. This is where you start with a broad idea. This broad request gives the AI a wide scope to generate a variety of unique and interesting ideas.

Here is a sample prompt:

Give me 20 high-concept pitches for a best-selling science fiction beach romance novel.

And here is part of the output from ChatGPT (I won't bore you with the whole thing):

1. *"Aquatic Hearts": When a marine biologist studying alien sea creatures on an exoplanet unexpectedly falls in love with an entity she can only communicate with via bioluminescent signals, she must make a tough choice between her home and the intriguing new world of underwater romance.*

2. *"Wavelengths of Love": In a near-future, where*

time-travel tourism is a booming industry, a lifeguard meets a woman from the distant future on his beach. They fall in love, but he realizes the only way to be with her is to leave his own timeline behind.

3. *"Beachy Cyborg": A robot designed to clean ocean pollution falls in love with an eco-activist. Together they navigate the blurry line between artificial intelligence and genuine emotion, challenging societal norms and their own understanding of love.*

From these options, select the one that resonates with you the most. This choice is the seed from which your story will grow. It's the high-level concept that you'll be drilling down into.

Another prompt that I like to use is the following based around Blake Snyder's description of a logline:

Give me 20 loglines for a GENRE story, in the style recommended by Blake Snyder that includes the following elements: The protagonist or main character, the context or setup of the story, what the main character wants or is trying to achieve, the antagonist or main obstacle facing the protagonist, the main conflict or problem that drives the story, and an ironic hook or twist that makes the concept intriguing. It

should be 25-30 words to concisely capture the essence of the story.

I'll go over some more brainstorming prompts like these later, but for now, this should give you an idea.

Step 2: Develop a Story Synopsis

Once you have your logline, the next step is to develop a story synopsis. This is where you start to add more detail to your concept. Ask the AI to develop a story synopsis based on your chosen concept. Here is my sample prompt:

Using the following concept, write a story synopsis for a bestselling science fiction beach romance book. Be sure to divide the story into three acts, and include the climax and ending of the book.

Concept: "Wavelengths of Love": In a near-future, where time-travel tourism is a booming industry, a lifeguard meets a woman from the distant future on his beach. They fall in love, but he realizes the only way to be with her is to leave his own timeline behind.

And here are the results:

Title: Wavelengths of Love

Act 1 - Meeting Across Time

In the near future, time-travel tourism has become a reality, changing the dynamic of Earth's tourist spots. Jack, a dedicated lifeguard at a popular beach in California, leads a simple, yet content life, valuing the daily rhythm of the tides more than the high-tech spectacle around him. One day, amidst the hustle and bustle of temporal tourists, he encounters Lyra, a mysterious and captivating woman who seems out of place, even amongst the time travelers.

They quickly develop a deep connection. Lyra, who's from a few centuries in the future, is fascinated by Jack's devotion to a bygone lifestyle, and Jack is intrigued by her blend of wisdom and naivety about his own time. Their shared evenings, filled with laughter, tales of different eras, and shared dreams under the timeless glow of the moonlight, lead to an unexpected romance.

Act 2 - A Future Apart

Their peaceful days come to an abrupt end when Lyra's time-travel permit nears expiration, forcing her to return to her era. Jack is left with a difficult choice: remain in his own time and lose Lyra forever or journey to a potentially unrecognizable future. Driven by love, Jack starts investigating the risky and complex procedure to become a future migrant, facing various hurdles, including time bureaucracy, stringent physical examinations, and the disapproval of his friends and family, who fear losing him forever.

Parallelly, Lyra returns to her era, her heart heavy with the knowledge of her separation from Jack. In her technologically advanced and utopian society, she starts feeling the weight of her decision. But she holds onto the hope that Jack might be able to join her in her time.

Act 3 - Tides of Time

Jack manages to overcome all the odds and gets approved to migrate to Lyra's timeline. As he prepares to leave everything he knows behind, his beach, now bustling with tourists from various eras, seems timeless, mirroring his feelings for Lyra

- a love that transcends time itself.

In the climactic sequence, Jack finally travels to the future, finding himself in a world that is vastly different yet strangely familiar. He struggles initially, feeling lost and out of place in the technological wonderland. But when he finally reunites with Lyra, his struggle seems worthwhile.

Ending

In the end, Jack finds that the rhythm of the tides he loved so much back in his own time still holds true, even in this futuristic world. With Lyra, he finds a new purpose, becoming a lifeguard once again, but this time, for an artificial beach that caters to tourists from the past. Jack and Lyra's love story becomes a symbol of timeless love across different eras, highlighting that the power of love can transcend the most enormous boundaries, even time itself.

At this stage, it's important to ensure that the synopsis aligns with your vision for the story. Read through it carefully and make any necessary adjustments. This might involve fixing plot holes, changing or adding characters, or tweaking the storyline. This is also a good time to start brainstorming characters and world-building. The more detail you can provide to the AI in the next steps, the better the output will be.

Step 3: Create an Outline

With a solid synopsis in hand, the next step is to create an outline. This is where you start to break down your story into manageable chunks. Ask the AI to develop a detailed outline based on the story framework of your choice. This will give you a clear roadmap for your story, with each step representing a key stage in your protagonist's journey.

Here is my sample prompt:

Using that synopsis, write a detailed 12-step outline based on the Hero's Journey framework as defined by Christopher Vogler.

And here are the results:

Title: Wavelengths of Love

1. Ordinary World: Jack is a lifeguard at a beach in California in the near future where time-travel tourism has become a reality. Despite the changing world, he enjoys his simple lifestyle and values the rhythm of the tides.

2. Call to Adventure: Lyra, a captivating woman from the future, arrives at the beach as a time-tourist. Jack feels an immediate connection with her.

3. Refusal of the Call: Although intrigued by Lyra, Jack is hesitant to pursue his feelings, aware that she comes from a different time and will eventually return there.

4. Meeting with the Mentor: Lyra encourages Jack to embrace the time differences and shares insights about her world, nurturing their bond and sparking a romantic relationship.

5. Crossing the Threshold: Their peaceful time comes to an end when Lyra's permit expires, forcing her to return to her era. Jack is left with the difficult choice of staying or trying to travel to Lyra's timeline.

6. Tests, Allies, Enemies: Jack faces many hurdles as he investigates time migration - the time-travel bureaucracy, health checks, and disapproval from his friends and family. Despite these challenges, his resolve only grows stronger.

7. Approach to the Inmost Cave: Jack receives approval for his time migration. He prepares to leave everything he knows behind, filled with anxiety about the future yet driven by his love for Lyra.

8. Ordeal: Jack arrives in the future, a world that is foreign yet eerily familiar. The challenge of acclimatization hits him hard, and he starts questioning his decision.

9. Reward: Jack reunites with Lyra, finding solace in their love. Despite the strangeness of the future world, their connection feels as natural as it did on the California beach.

10. The Road Back: Jack tries to fit into the new world, often finding himself struggling. But he's determined to create a life here with Lyra.

11. Resurrection: Jack finds a position as a lifeguard at an artificial beach in the future, serving tourists from the past. This role brings a sense of normalcy and purpose to his life in the future.

12. Return with the Elixir: Jack's love story with Lyra becomes a symbol of timeless love in the futuristic society. Their tale signifies that love can transcend time and space, proving the power of human connection despite massive differences. Jack's journey from his past to the future serves as a beacon of hope, adaptation, and timeless love.

At this stage, you should have a clear idea of the overall structure of your story. Each step in the outline represents a chapter or a key event in the story. This is the skeleton of your story, providing a framework that you'll flesh out in the next step.

Step 4: Develop Story Beats

Story beats are the specific action and emotional points that happen throughout a chapter. They're the most important part of this step, because bad beats will result in bad output in the prose. For each chapter, ask the AI to create a detailed outline with a certain number of story beats (I go with 12-20).

Here is a sample prompt for the first chapter in this example:

Using the following chapter summary, create a detailed outline for the chapter with 12 story beats. They delve deeper into the specific action and emotional beats that happen throughout the entire chapter:

Ordinary World: Jack is a lifeguard at a beach in California in the near future where time-travel tourism has become a reality. Despite the changing world, he enjoys his simple lifestyle and values the rhythm of the tides.

And here are the results:

Chapter 1: The Timeless Tide

Beat 1: Introduction to Jack's character, portraying him as a lifeguard devoted to his job at the beach in California. Establish his role, dedication, and strong sense of responsibility.

Beat 2: Jack observes the morning rituals of the beach - opening the lifeguard station, setting up the beach warning signs, watching the first of the tourists arriving.

Beat 3: Introduction of time-travel tourism. Jack watches as a group of time-travel tourists materialize onto the beach, showcasing the futuristic aspects of his world.

Beat 4: Despite the technological advancement, Jack shows a preference for his simple lifestyle. He scans the ocean with binoculars, appreciating the timeless rhythm of the waves.

Beat 5: A close call on the beach leads to Jack performing a successful rescue, demonstrating his capability as a lifeguard and his commitment to his work.

Beat 6: After the rescue, Jack interacts with the crowd and the rescued tourist, showing his personality - calm, kind, but somewhat reserved, avoiding unnecessary attention.

Beat 7: As the day goes by, Jack witnesses various other time-travel tourists arrive and depart, demonstrating the transient nature of his beach. This highlights the difference between his static lifestyle and the dynamic, ever-changing tourist populace.

Beat 8: Jack shares an intimate moment with the beach, showcasing his deep bond with the sea and his job. His musings reveal his appreciation of the tides, drawing a parallel with his own life.

Beat 9: Jack ends his day at work, cleaning and packing up. His reflections about the day and the events serve as a metaphor for his existence - an anchor in the midst of the changing tides of time.

Beat 10: Jack returns home to his modest beach house, emphasizing his choice to live a simple life despite the high-tech world around him.

Beat 11: Jack spends his evening on the porch, watching the sun set over the ocean, further establishing his deep connection with the beach and the sea.

Beat 12: As night falls, Jack retires, setting up for the next day. He expresses a feeling of contentment with his life, unaware of the changes that are about to come, setting the stage for the ensuing story.

Each story beat should represent a specific event or emotional point in the chapter. They should be detailed enough to give a clear sense of what happens, but broad enough to allow for some flexibility in the actual writing. At this stage, you're not writing the chapter yet, but rather setting the stage for the action and emotion that will unfold.

This is also the stage where I would stop and do the most editing, to ensure that the beats represent exactly what you want to happen in the chapter.

Remember, if you don't specify, it won't be in the output. Be specific.

Step 5: Write the Chapter

Finally, with your story beats in hand, it's time to write the chapter. Ask the AI to write a chapter based on the story beats. The amount of output I target depends on the program I am using. With some programs, I'm able to utilize a "super prompt" that can get much more in-depth.

When I first created the example used in this chapter, I was using ChatGPT, and this is the super prompt I used (note that this is a relatively simple prompt):

Write 600 words of a chapter based on the following two story beats, and using the following details:

Genre: science fiction beach romance

Tone: lighthearted

Point of View: first person point of view from [CHARACTER's] perspective

Beat 1: Introduction to Jack's character, portraying him as a lifeguard devoted to his job at the beach in California. Establish his role, dedication, and strong sense of responsibility.

Beat 2: Jack observes the morning rituals of the beach - opening the lifeguard station, setting up the beach warning signs, watching the first of the tourists arriving.

And here are the results:

If there's one thing in life that grounds me, it's the rhythm of the Pacific Ocean, eternally pounding against the sun-bleached sands of our California beach. I'm Jack, by the way, your friendly neighborhood lifeguard and, in this ever-evolving world of time-hopping tourists, I'm a bit of an old soul.

Ever since I was a kid, I wanted to be a lifeguard. Not for the tan or the prestige, but for the very simple reason of preserving the sanctity of life against the untamed power of the sea. Yeah, I know. Quite the romantic, right? But here I am, whistle round my neck, zinc on my nose, fulfilling my child-

hood dream in the near-future where time-travel tourism is the latest fad.

My day begins early, the sky a soft blush as the dawn makes its grand appearance. The lifeguard station, my second home, is a humble building with a charm that contrasts with the flashy time-pods that sparkle in the morning sun. I unlock the door, run a hand along the worn-out map of our coastline, and smile. This, right here, is where I'm supposed to be.

Setting up the beach warning signs is a ritual I have honed to near perfection. I handle each sign with care, planting them in their designated spots, respecting the voiceless contract between me, the beach, and the ocean. Their messages vary - riptides here, jellyfish there - but they all say one thing clearly: respect the sea, for she is a powerful mistress.

Just as I finish my task, the soft hum of a time-pod punctuates the morning tranquility. A group of tourists from some future era, materialize out of thin air, their eyes wide with excitement. It's a sight that would've unsettled me years ago, but now it's just a part of the job.

They rush past me, not noticing the man in red shorts and the white tank top. To them, I'm part of the scenery, like the palm trees or the seagulls, a fixture of this era. And that suits me just fine. My role isn't to be a tour guide, but a guardian of their safety.

Their holographic swimsuits shimmer in the morning light, a stark contrast to the natural hues around us. Even as they hurry to experience our 'quaint' beach, I can't help but marvel at the beauty of this encounter, the meeting of different times on the same, unchanging shore.

From the highest point on my watchtower, I scan the horizon, binoculars in hand. The tourists splash around the shallows, their laughter a symphony that intertwines with the whispering waves. It's in moments like these that I truly understand my purpose: to ensure that every memory made here is a happy one, unmarred by the potential dangers of the ocean.

So, with the sun cresting over the horizon, I begin my day, ever watchful, ever ready. I can't predict what today, or any day, will bring. I can't control

the tides or the time travelers. But this is my world,
my beach, and I am its humble, devoted lifeguard.

And as you can see, we've got a much better output then we would have done had we just asked it to write the opening chapter of a science fiction beach romance (I made that genre up, by the way, feel free to grab it now while it's hot).

Now I hope I haven't overwhelmed you yet, because it really is a lot simpler once you start to try it. And don't worry, I've got a whole chapter about each of these steps, as well as a few other important steps, so you can really figure out what works for you, and take a careful approach to writing fiction with AI, one that should result in far higher-quality output than you would have had otherwise.

Additionally, many programs like Novelcrafter or Sudowrite have built-in mechanics that make crafting these prompts a lot easier.

Tips for Success with the Fractal Technique

The Fractal Technique is a powerful tool for writing with AI, but like any tool, it requires skill and practice to use effectively. Here are some tips to help you get the most out of this technique:

- **Edit as You Go**: As you progress through each step, make sure to edit and refine the output. This will ensure that the final product aligns with your vision.

Don't be afraid to make changes or adjustments as needed. Remember that if you don't steer it in the right direction for *each* step, it will be much harder to revise in the end.

- **Add Detail**: Don't be afraid to add detail to your prompts. In fact, this is crucial. You want to have specifics, otherwise the AI will have rather vague output. This is why it's important to edit as you go, to make sure that you have the right details to draw from in future steps.

- **Iterate and Improve**: If the AI's output isn't quite right, tweak your prompt and try again. The more you do this, the better your prompts will become, and the less editing you'll need to do.

Alright! That is this entire book in a nutshell. You can stop reading now!

Just kidding.

Obviously, there are a lot more skills to refine along the way, which is why the bulk of the book to come is all about each step of the writing process, and some of my favorite prompts to get the most out of the AI as you go.

The Fractal Technique is just to provide you with the steps to take when writing fiction. You always want to start with the idea, move on to the synopsis, etc.

In the next chapter, we'll cover brainstorming, one of the areas where AI excels the most.

Summary:

- The "Fractal Technique" is a method for writing fiction that starts with just the initial idea, then drilling down into more detail.

- It involves a minimum of five steps:

  - Generating your ideas

  - Developing the synopsis

  - Creating an outline

  - Developing specific story beats

  - Writing the actual chapters

- You'll want to edit as you go to get the best results

9

BRAINSTORMING

One of my first attempts at a YouTube channel was an utter failure. I had wanted to create an instructional hub for authors that went over every possible step in intricate detail, from brainstorming to the finished product. I was going to do in-depth "seasons" for each step of the process, starting with brainstorming.

Well that idea didn't turn out great (basically I was giving myself too much work, and limiting myself to a specific structure rather than experimenting to see what people actually wanted to watch).

But what I did get out of those first few episodes I produced was a great appreciation of brainstorming.

Because there are so many cool ways to do it!

Now, brainstorming is really just a process of finding a bunch of little puzzle pieces and putting them together in original and interesting ways. Most people think that books run on a single great idea, but really it's a huge collage of ideas, and they vary from initial concepts, to characters, settings, conflicts, plot twists, you name it.

So there's a lot to cover here.

Basically what I will teach you in this chapter are the underlying principles on how to brainstorm with AI, enough that you'll have a good idea of what to do when you're short an idea.

Because even if you think you already know what your book will be about, I guarantee there are holes in the puzzle that you haven't figured out yet. And you'll need to brainstorm for that.

Keep in mind that we are not trying to go deep here. We're not going to flesh out an entire character's backstory, or the political history of your fictional nation. All we want are the initial ideas and a decent sense of how they fit together.

So let's get started.

The Initial Concept

If you're anything like me, this step might be one you can skip, because you already have a huge wealth of ideas, and you don't need AI to get you started on any of them. However, since this book is meant to be thorough, here are a few prompts I use to generate that initial idea that gets the book started:

> **Give me [NUMBER] high-concept pitch-
> es for a bestselling [GENRE] story with a
> unique twist, intriguing characters, and
> gripping emotional stakes.**

> **Give me [NUMBER] ideas for characters
> that are part of a bestselling [GENRE] sto-
> ry that are well fleshed out, have strengths
> and weaknesses, and undergo conflict
> throughout the course of the story. Briefly
> describe their character arc.**

Most people start with either a plot-focused concept, or
a character-focused concept, which is why I would usually
start with either of these two prompt.

There's also great power in a simple logline, which has a
good blend of both plot AND character. And my prompt for
one of those looks like this:

> **Give me 20 loglines for a GENRE story,
> in the style recommended by Blake Sny-
> der that includes the following elements:
> The protagonist or main character, the con-
> text or setup of the story, what the main
> character wants or is trying to achieve,
> the antagonist or main obstacle facing the**

protagonist, the main conflict or problem that drives the story, and an ironic hook or twist that makes the concept intriguing. It should be 25-30 words to concisely capture the essence of the story.

Bear in mind that a lot of the output that ChatGPT or Claude will give you are generic and not very good. But remember my chapter on collaboration. You have to learn to dig deeper. Ask follow up questions, use what it gave you as inspiration, then feed it your own input based on what it inspired you to add. I've found that even generic and bad answers (in the brainstorming phase) often still help get my creative juices flowing, because it gets me thinking about what I DON'T want to do, which helps me narrow down what I DO want to do.

When You Already Know the Initial Concept

If you already have an idea of what you want to write, or are ready to move on from the initial concept above, but want to expand upon it, here is the prompt I would start with:

I'd like to write a [GENRE] novel about [YOUR IDEA]. Please help me expand on this idea by providing potential details about interesting protagonists, antago-

nists, side characters, settings, plot twists, and subplots. Make a list of 100 possibilities.

If you have specific ideas already formed about the setting, characters, etc. be sure to mention that as well.

The reason I ask it to give me 100 possibilities, is to force the AI to be brief with its ideas, to stretch its limits of creativity, and to just get a TON of ideas on the table. Good brainstorming is all about getting as many ideas down as possible, then eliminating the bad ones.

The What-If Game

One of my favorite ways to brainstorm is to play, "What if". This can be with anything you want. For example, one of my ideas is "What if an older Sherlock Holmes teamed up with other pulp heroes to fight Cthulhu?" which led to a novella I'm currently writing with AI.

The key is to start with something mundane or familiar to people, then add a "what if" to make it more interesting. Here's how I would prompt the AI:

I'd like you to create a list of "What if" statements related to [YOUR ORDINARY THING] to be used in a [GENRE] story. Please give me [NUMBER] possibilities.

You can adapt this prompt for a variety of settings. For instance, giving you a list of existing stories that would make a good transition to your genre. Like asking it to give you ideas for a sci-fi version of Harry Potter.

The First Line

One technique that a lot of people use to brainstorm a book idea (one that might be useful to you discovery writers out there) is to create the first line first, then develop the story from there. Here's the prompt I would use:

> **Give me a list of [NUMBER] potential first lines for a [GENRE] novel. The line should include at least one character, include some kind of conflict, and should be quick, engaging, and action-oriented to hook the reader.**

News Stories

There are tons of interesting news stories out there. And it's not just true crime either. You can easily take an existing news story and ask the AI to adapt it to any genre. I often like to take existing military news and have the AI adapt it to a science fiction story, for example. When combined in these interesting ways, you end up getting some pretty wacky and fun ideas. Here's the prompt I would use:

> **Using the following news story, brainstorm [NUMBER] ideas for a [GENRE] book: [PASTE NEWS STORY HERE]**

Alternatively, with AI programs like ChatGPT (with it's ability to read the web) or Perplexity, you could also literally paste in the url of the news story, and ChatGPT would be able to read it that way, rather than have you paste the entire news story text into the chat.

I also like to ask the AI for made-up sample news stories from my existing world. That prompt could go something like this:

> **Come up with [NUMBER] news article teasers covering unusual events, crimes, disasters or discoveries that could drive the plot of a [GENRE] story.**

If you already know your genre, you might adapt that prompt to be more appropriate. For example, with a true crime novel, you could ask for a sample police report.

Job Titles

People like to read about interesting people.

That's why looking through a list of job titles is a great way to brainstorm a main character. You can Google a list of interesting professions, or simply ask the AI for a list of possibilities. Here's a good prompt for that:

> **Give me a list of interesting and unusual professions that one might find in a [INSERT A SETTING OR GENRE] setting.**

Once you have an occupation you like, you can then move on to expanding your story around that character and their occupation.

> **Please brainstorm a list of plot, character, setting, and theme ideas for a [GENRE] book where the protagonist is a [OCCUPATION].**

Would You Rather

When my wife and I were first married, we loved to play the game "Would You Rather". Which isn't so much a game, as just a fun series of questions that give you ridiculous choices. Well, it's ridiculous choices like these that can really get the creative juices flowing, and provide unique sources of conflict that could be valuable for a story.

So whenever I'm brainstorming a book idea, and this also works well for plot twists, I will sometimes use a prompt like this:

Give me [NUMBER] ridiculous "Would You Rather" scenario questions related to a [GENRE] book about [YOUR CONCEPT].

Alternatively, you could just leave off the "Your Concept" part, and just have it give you ideas related to your genre (though I recommend you be specific with the subgenre). Even if the results aren't something you would base a whole story around, it can often give you some good ideas for plot twists or unique character/worldbuilding quirks.

This Meets That

One of the best ways to produce seemingly original ideas (emphasis on *seemingly*), is to mash up two or more ideas. I've sort of touched on this in the "What If" section, but sometimes you can just give it two or more ideas and have it brainstorm various mashups. Sometimes the ideas it spits out are golden! Here is a sample prompt:

Brainstorm [NUMBER] book ideas, using a plausible mashup of [THING 1], [THING 2], [THING 3], etc...

Or, let's say you only have one thing, and you want to mash it up with another thing, but you don't know what that second thing is. You could ask the AI to generate a list of media in a preferred genre or type, then have the AI combine that with your initial idea.

There are honestly a lot of ways that you could go about this.

A Social Issue

Many of us get into writing because we have a message we want to share with the world. And while we always want to avoid getting preachy (which tends to have the opposite effect of what we want), it's important to keep our values close while writing. And they can honestly make for great ideas.

If you have a social issue or other value that you want to provide commentary on through story, but you don't know exactly what form that should take, here's a prompt I would use to brainstorm:

I'd like to write a book involving the social issue/value/theme of [INSERT ISSUE

HERE], please brainstorm [NUMBER] ideas for a [GENRE] book that can incorporate this issue in a way that is meaningful yet subtle. Make sure the concept is not too preachy, and fully explores the issue from multiple angles.

Summarizing it All

Whoo! That's a lot of brainstorming we've been doing there. But ultimately, we need a succinct way to sum up our story. And so for this last section, I'd like to show you how you can do that, and how AI could help.

Personally, I like the "Who/Who Must" framework. I first learned about this from taking a course by James Scott Bell, a notable educator of bestselling fiction. He says that every story is essentially about a character taking action, and so he lays out the "Who/Who Must" framework as something like this: **My story is about BLANK who must BLANK in order to BLANK.**

That's every bestselling story in a nutshell. You have character, and that character must take action in order to achieve what they desire.

You could also adapt my Blake Snyder logline prompt above to do much the same thing, because it is very similar.

Thankfully, AI loves a good framework.

By this point, I'm hopeful that you have a lot of good ideas and thoughts that you've saved. So what I would do is round up all of the ideas you've got, trim away anything that is no longer relevant, then use this prompt:

> **I'd like you to create a short pitch for a story using all of the information below. Sum it up in using this framework: My story is about BLANK who must BLANK in order to BLANK. Give me a list of [NUMBER] options.**
>
> **[INSERT ALL YOUR STORY INFO HERE]**

Summary:

- Use AI to brainstorm, allowing it to fill the gaps in your initial concept and construct a network of initial ideas.

- Utilize different brainstorming methods with AI, such as creating the initial concept or iterating off an existing concept, using news stories, job titles, and "What-If" and "Would You Rather" games.

- Incorporate social issues or values subtly into your story for a meaningful narrative; use AI to brainstorm around these issues.

- Summarize your ideas using the "Who/Who Must" pitch framework: My story is about BLANK who must BLANK in order to BLANK.

10

GENRE/TROPE RESEARCH

One of my early mentors in self-publishing (though he probably doesn't know who I am) was Chris Fox. I still remember the day I read his first book for authors, 5000 Words an Hour. I literally couldn't sleep that night, realizing what was possible.

Boy, if I could go back in time and tell my younger self about what would eventually be possible with AI.

But another of Chris' books that has been hugely influential is his book: Write to Market.

In it, this book outlines why it's important to know the market, to be well read in your market, and to include the right tropes to meet the expectations of readers.

This has gone on to be a bit controversial among authors, especially among those who say that you shouldn't have to "give in" to market demands.

I tend to fall somewhere in the middle of these arguments. I will personally never write a book that I'm not interested in.

But at the same time, I tend to be interested in ideas that are easily marketable with a little massaging.

But one thing I can get behind, and that is doing research. Because the more you can know about your target audience, the more you are likely to appeal to them (which means more books sold).

The best way to research your genre is by reading books in a genre, and getting to know the reader communities around those genres.

But if I had to pick the second best way, it would be to do your research with AI.

Because AI is actually pretty good at this.

I even tested some more niche and modern genres like progression fantasy and reverse harem romance, and it knew a lot about each (more than I did about the latter, in fact).

But when working with the AI, we want to be able to get the best results, results that we can actively put to use in a story.

By now, you should have brainstormed your initial idea, but you might not have fully fleshed out characters or a detailed plot yet. You're still forming your ideas, which means this is the perfect time to interject a few tropes in there. This way, you can really appeal to your target market.

First, Get a List of Genres

If you don't know what genre fits your story best, then the first step is to figure that out. It will make marketing much easier for you down the road.

Here is the prompt I would start with:

Please make me a list all of the different subgenres and sub-sub genres of [BROAD GENRE HERE]. The list should have at least 100 entries.

The broad genre is usually something along the lines of Romance, Thriller, Horror, Fantasy, Science Fiction, Mystery, etc. And I ask it for 100 entries, because you want it to really think of every possibility. If you ask it for 10 options, it will give you the ten most broad. You can ask it for more than 100 too.

Side note: I found that both ChatGPT and Claude performed equally well at this task. Both returned results that I was not expecting when I asked it to list 100 fantasy genres. Some of the options were not real genres, but it got a few that I didn't think it would get, like Noblebright Fantasy, Portal Fantasy or Progression Fantasy.

Ask the AI What it Knows About the Genre

The next step is to ask the AI what it knows. I like to do it this way, because you will start to get a sense of the building blocks of your genre, and you get a chance to see what the AI will be able to intuitively know about your genre.

Also, let's say you have a specific genre that you know exists, but that you don't see on a list that the AI generates. In that case, I simply check to make sure the AI knows what the genre is.

In either case, the prompt goes like this:

> **What do you know about [SPECIFIC GENRE]?**

You can then see what it gives you and ask follow up questions if needed.

Ask the AI for a List of Tropes

Now we get into the list of tropes, which is where things can get fun. Start with a prompt like this:

> **Can you provide me with a comprehensive list of at least [NUMBER] tropes associated with [SPECIFIC GENRE]?**

Generally, a list of 20-30 tropes is sufficient. I don't like to ask it for too many here, as I don't want it to make up a ton of tropes just to fill the quota. You can even take out the number all together if you want, then ask it for more if it didn't give you enough. Asking the AI for more options is almost always a good way to get deeper results.

Now the real trick is to take those tropes and find a way to integrate them into your story. Some of them will appear obvious, but there may be others that don't. So don't hesitate to ask the AI for ideas with a prompt like this:

Please brainstorm [NUMBER] different ways to incorporate [TROPES] into the following story idea: [PASTE STORY IDEA HERE]

Who knows, it might be easier than you think to incorporate all those tropes.

Generate a List of Necessary Scenes

Last but not least, we want to generate a list of scenes or chapters that are unique to your specific genre, and that you will want to include in your overall outline later.

So one of the terms that those of us in the AI community have found to be helpful is this concept of "Obligatory Scenes", which seems to be a term that the AI likes. The prompt goes something like this:

Please provide me with a comprehensive list of obligatory scenes for a [SPECIFIC GENRE] novel.

Once it gives you the list, you should probably ask it if there are any more, and it will spit out a few more that you need.

This is one of those tips that I think might be obsolete once newer models come along, but for now, asking for obligatory scenes seems to get good results. However, I've often found that asking the AI for a list of "necessary scenes" for a specific genre often works just as well.

Why do you want this?

Because every genre usually has these scenes that are specific to that genre, and that you will want to include in your writing. These are similar but often different from tropes. For example, a thriller usually has a scene where the villain has the hero completely at their mercy. This is something that wouldn't necessarily come up in the list of tropes, but you would want to have in a list of necessary scenes.

Once you've got a solid list of these scenes, you'll want to trim that list to include the ones you want to use, and then you can plug that list into your prompts in later chapters when we're outlining. This will result in a much richer outline.

I'll have more to say about Obligatory Scenes in the chapter on Outlining.

Summary:

- Get a comprehensive list of genres and subgenres from the AI to find the best fit. Ask for at least 100.

- Ask the AI what it knows about your chosen genre to gauge its knowledge. Follow up with more questions.

- Request a list of common tropes associated with the genre and brainstorm ways to incorporate them.

- Ask for a list of obligatory scenes typical for the genre to include later in your outline.

- Trim the scene list down to the ones you want to use when outlining to ensure your book hits the expected story beats.

11

SYNOPSIS

Alright, we've already made a lot of progress so far, but now it's time to dig into the next step of the Fractal Method process, which is developing the synopsis.

Now, for you discovery writers out there, you can just skip this step, and move on to the story beats, or even writing the prose. But for outliners, I usually like to have a solid overall synopsis of my whole story before I start digging deep into the characters and the worldbuilding.

I debated talking about the synopsis later, when we get to the chapter on outlining, but really this is a step that should be done before you flesh out worldbuilding and characters, so you can take all of that together to help inform your outline.

In other words, you need at least a basic story structure to really help you know what you need to worldbuild/research, as well as what your character arcs will look like.

That said, fiction is a fickle thing. You'll probably find yourself going back and forth on a lot of these things. Regardless, I think this chapter on the Synopsis is best served here.

Anyway...

Building a Synopsis Prompt

By now, you should have a bunch of brainstormed...stuff, for lack of a better term. A lot of that stuff will probably involve your premise, it may involve your ending, along with certain scenes that may happen in the middle. It also probably involves some of the characters, and maybe some of the most relevant worldbuilding.

It looks different for everybody.

You're going to need all of this for the synopsis, but I usually like to start with...

The Ending First

This is a clever trick for working with AI: starting with the end in mind.

Why?

Because we have to remember that AI is a predictive model, meaning it works almost exactly the way the predictive text on your phone works. With each word it writes, it's using probability to decide what word makes the most sense to put next. And if it doesn't know where it's going, each word, each sentence, each paragraph, is likely to go in wildly unpredictable directions.

However, if it knows where you are going, it's much more likely that all of the plotting it gives you in between is likely to turn out to be much more focused and targeted. And it might even include some subtle foreshadowing of the ending in earlier chapters.

So when you're starting to create your synopsis, I always like to start with the ending. Of course, if you already know the ending, you can skip this step, otherwise, use a prompt like this:

> **Given the following premise and story information, give me [NUMBER] possible endings to this [GENRE] novel.**
>
> **[INSERT PREMISE AND RELEVANT BRAINSTORMING INFORMATION HERE]**

It will then give you a list of endings to choose from.

Building the Synopsis

Once you know your ending, here is the prompt I would use to craft the entire synopsis:

Given the following premise and story information, give me a highly detailed synopsis for a [GENRE] story in the traditional three act structure.

Premise:

Ending:

Other Information:

This should lead to a detailed synopsis that may be the most solidified your story has been so far. Congrats! This is where I start to get excited about what AI can do for me.

However, you can't stop here.

Fix Up the Synopsis

The last step is to edit the synopsis to be exactly what you want, because AI isn't always perfect. You may find there are specific details that you want to include. And in fact, I would look for areas where it seems overly vague and add those details in yourself.

DO NOT SKIP THIS STEP!

This is a step you will need to do at each major piece of the process. If you don't include the specific information you want in the finished novel, it will not appear there.

Now, admittedly, we're still only at the synopsis phase here, so you don't have to get too specific...yet.

But you do want to make sure any major plot arcs are included in this synopsis. And this may also be a good time to identify the major arc of your subplot(s) and/or main character across all three acts and include those as well.

If you think of writing with AI like building a house, this is the step where you're laying the foundation of the house. So you will need to know where all of the rooms are going to go, and what size they should be. We're not actually building the rooms yet, but if we don't lay out space for them in the floor plan, those rooms won't exist.

Summary:

- Start with the ending first when creating a synopsis, as this helps the AI stay focused when filling in the middle. Prompt the AI for possible endings if you don't already have one in mind.

- Once you have an ending, prompt the AI to generate a full synopsis with beginning, middle, and end in a three act structure. Make sure major plot points are included.

- Edit the AI-generated synopsis to add any missing details you want to be sure to include. Flesh out any areas that seem too vague.

- The synopsis is like the foundation of your story. If details aren't included here, they won't make it into the final novel.

- You can iterate back and forth between the synopsis, worldbuilding, and characters to refine each part.

- Don't skip editing the AI output at each step. This is crucial for getting the details you want in the final story.

12

Worldbuilding and Research

When I was writing my first book series, I thought worldbuilding had to do with creating magic systems, new races, epic cultures, and more of that sort of thing.

And while it is that, I was surprised at what I didn't know about worldbuilding. For instance, EVERY genre needs worldbuilding.

Yes, I mean that. Worldbuilding isn't just for fantasy and sci-fi authors.

Because worldbuilding is about more than fantasy races or new technologies. It could be as simple as planning out the layout of the room a scene takes place in.

Seriously, you don't know how many times I've had to pause my writing so I could map out the location where my characters are standing.

That's worldbuilding. You might also hear it referred to more simply as "setting."

But for contemporary or historical novels, you will also have to do research.

Research serves the same function as worldbuilding, but with the one distinction that the information is already out there and must be collected, as opposed to worldbuilding where you just make it up as you go.

(I'll let you decide which one is easier.)

So let's take a brief look at each of these and ways that AI can help. I don't have specific prompts to work with on this chapter because most of these prompts will simple be asking the AI for ideas or for information. There aren't really any specific prompting tactics to make the worldbuilding easier, but I do have a list of things you should brainstorm for inspiration.

Worldbuilding Assistance

When it comes to building a believable fictional world, AI collaboration can enhance virtually every aspect of the process. Let's explore some of the key ways step-by-step:

First, AI excels at generating fresh ideas and possibilities to inspire your worldbuilding. Say you want to design an original setting but feel stuck - you can simply describe the vague notion in your head to the AI. Maybe you envision a seaside city, an underground colony, a space station...what ever sparks your creativity. The AI will quickly offer a number of unique directions to explore.

From there, you can choose an idea that intrigues you and prompt the AI to expand on it. Want help mapping out the city districts, the political factions, the architectural styles? The AI can flesh out the concept into finely-tuned details, allowing you to visualize the setting more clearly. You might find some details that you would have never thought of.

Here are some key elements to consider including in a worldbuilding sheet or guide:

- **Geography** - Continents, major landforms, bodies of water, climate etc. Brainstorming for maps can be helpful.

- **Nations/Governments** - Names, political systems, relationships between different groups.

- **Technology Level** - Overall feel of scientific advancement in areas like medicine, transportation, weapons, communications.

- **Architecture/Infrastructure** - Building materials and styles, city layouts, types of roads.

- **Culture & Society** - Religions, family structures, gender roles/norms, leisure activities, art forms.

- **Rituals & Customs** - Ceremonies for birth, death, coming of age, weddings etc. As well as smaller customs.

- **Languages** - Written scripts, common phrases, names for places/people/items.

- **Economy & Trade** - Currency, imports/exports, industries, natural resources.

- **History Overview** - Major historical events, power shifts, noteworthy figures. Recent past vs ancient.

- **Magic/Supernatural Elements** - Sources, limits, costs, abilities, rituals, artifacts etc.

- **Flora & Fauna** - Unique fantasy plants/animals or real variations.

- **Character Profiles** - Names, physical descriptions, backgrounds, abilities, personalities.

- **Factions/Groups** - Religious sects, guilds, military orders, noble houses, criminal syndicates.

- **Laws & Crime** - Legal codes, punishments, law enforcement groups, corruption.

- **Mythology & Lore** - Stories, prophecies, creatures, heroes/villains important to the culture.

The depth of each item can vary based on your needs. Start broad, then expand areas that impact your story most.

Don't be afraid to give the AI very open-ended prompts. Say you're struggling for ideas on how magic could work in your world. Simply ask the AI to pitch some original magic systems along with details on abilities, limits and costs.

Comb through the results for inspiration or even combine elements from multiple ideas into your own hybrid system.

Research Assistance

Besides igniting bold worldbuilding ideas, AI can serve as an invaluable research companion for fiction writers. Its ability to swiftly analyze massive amounts of information allows you to efficiently deepen your knowledge on whatever topics you need to make your story world feel real.

Let's say you want a quick primer on quantum physics to plausibly incorporate into a sci-fi tale. Simply ask the AI to provide an overview summary, and it will synthesize the most relevant details into a digestible explanation, much more efficient than skimming multiple articles yourself. The AI can deliver these abbreviated packages on nearly any subject.

Need to check a historical detail for accuracy? AI excels at lightning-fast fact checking. Unsure if the firearm or idiom you mentioned fits the time period? Feed it the specifics and it will validate or correct you in seconds. The AI becomes an omniscient reference librarian at your fingertips.

Speaking of history, accurately depicting past eras provides crucial texture to many fictional works. Here the AI can dig up obscure historical information to make your worldbuilding truly authentic. Have it research medieval fashion, colonial occupation practices, sailing terminology - anything that grounds your audience in past time period. The depth of its historical knowledge far surpasses a human's.

Here are some key topics that could be useful to research for contemporary or historical fiction novels:

- **Time Period Details** - Politics, major news events, popular culture, technology of the era.

- **Locations** - Geography, architecture, local culture, climate, dialects if real places.

- **Social Issues** - Attitudes and norms around gender, race, class, sexuality etc.

- **Daily Life** - Fashion, food, homes, occupations, education, transportation, health practices.

- **Warfare** - Weaponry, military tactics, major conflicts, impacts on society.

- **Law & Government** - Political systems, law enforcement, justice system, social services.

- **Economy** - Industries, trade, wages, costs of goods, class divides.

- **Science & Technology** - Major innovations, discoveries, inventions that shaped the era.

- **Art, Music & Literature** - Popular styles and notable works.

- **Religion** - Dominant faiths, rituals, tensions between belief systems.

- **Language** - Slang, turns of phrase, etiquette of communication.

- **Major Historical Figures** - Influential leaders, creators, pioneers.

- **Mythology & Folklore** - Stories and beliefs that permeate the culture.

- **Natural World** - Impacts of weather, pandemics, natural disasters.

Again, focus on researching detail areas that are most relevant to your particular story and characters. Create an immersive historical texture.

Now, there is a BIG caveat to this stage as opposed to worldbuilding, and that is the fact that the AI can often make mistakes. In other words, you could ask it for information about the ancient Celts, and it might give you something about the Anglo-Saxons, because in the mind of the AI, they are statistically similar. So it can get its wires crossed.

That is why it's important that you verify everything it tells you.

HOWEVER, there are going to be certain areas of research where you're not going to be able to verify it exactly, especially when it comes to small details surrounding an ancient culture, for example. Those details aren't necessarily something anyone today would know. But this is actually a good opportunity for the AI to shine, because it's really good at extrapolating. Once it understands the context, or you give it the research information it needs, you can ask it to postulate additional details that you can't find in the research.

Because let's face it, who really knows what it was like to live a long time ago, especially in ancient civilizations where we have very little to go on.

Begin with Setting

I always like to start fleshing out my setting with worldbuilding and/or research first, before I make much progress on anything else.

Why?

Because the setting does a LOT to inform all of the other elements.

For example, a character will act totally different in a historical France setting when compared to a modern-day Japan setting. They will talk differently, have a different level of education, fashion choices, opinions on social issues, etc.

So before we go any further in fleshing out the characters, the plot, and more, let's get that setting nailed down first.

Summary:

- Worldbuilding involves more than just fantasy/science fiction elements - every genre benefits from building out setting details.

- For contemporary/historical fiction, research is ideal to accurately depict past eras or real-world facts.

- AI can generate ideas for fictional worldbuilding elements like cultures, magic systems, etc.

- AI can also research real-world historical details, summarize topics, and extrapolate plausible details.

- However, AI research should be verified for accuracy - AI can sometimes get details crossed.

- It's best to start with developing the setting first, as it informs other elements like characters, plot, dialogue.

13

CHARACTERS

Characters are one of the few areas where the approach with AI is a little different than the way things used to be done.

Before, when you were fleshing out a character, you would usually create a detailed profile of that character, then chart exactly what that character's arc might look like over the course of the novel.

And don't get me wrong, we still need to do those things.

But there are a couple of other extra steps that I really enjoyed discovering as I worked with various LLMs. One of them, in particular, kind of blew my mind when I first discovered what it can do.

But before we get to those fun hacks, let's talk about how we fully flesh out these characters for ourselves.

The Character Profile

The character profile is not something that every writer uses, but many do, and it can be a good way to really wrap your head around that character. Plus, fleshing out a good character is the first step to getting that character ready to use in AI.

But one of the reasons why I think many authors don't bother to create a character profile is because it can take so much time, and you'll end up defining a lot of information that might not seem to matter on the surface.

Thankfully, AI is GREAT at filling out plausible character profiles.

Now, I have a big prompt here, but mostly because I've designed it to contain just about any part of a character profile that you might need. You can feel free to add to or remove any part from the template. But this is what I would give the AI to start my character profile sheet:

You are an expert at crafting well-rounded, dynamic characters. We're going to create a character profile for the [protagonist/antagonist/mentor/etc.] of my [GENRE] book. The finished profile should be 1500 words long. Here is what I know so far about the character:

[INSERT YOUR KNOWN DETAILS HERE]

With that information in mind, build a character profile that includes highly detailed information on the following:

Basic Details: Name, Age, Place of Birth, Current Residence, Nationality, Education Level, Occupation, Income Level, Marital Status.

Physical Attributes: Height, Weight, Build, Skin Color, Eye Color, Hair Color, Face Shape, Distinguishing marks like tattoos/scars/birthmarks/etc., Any Physical Ailments or Disfigurements.

Clothing and Style: What do they typically wear? (at work, out on the town, at home, asleep, etc.) Do they wear accessories of any kind? Are there any objects or pets that they keep close? What is their level of grooming? (disheveled, neat, wearing makeup, etc.)

Communication and Mannerisms: Are they from a foreign land? What is their posture? (stiff, slouching, casual, relaxed, exhausted, etc.) Do they have a specific gesture that they overuse? (hand-talking, controlled, agitated) Do they make eye contact with the people they talk to? What curse word do they use the most? Do they curse? Do they have a catch phrase? Do they have speech impediments? Are there any "ticks" in the way they talk/move? What does their laugh sound like? (loud and booming, snickering, high squeak) What is their handwriting like? How do they walk? (confident, lazy, fast, distracted, etc.) What is their smile like? (warm, false, nervous, etc.) Do they wear their emotions on their sleeve or keep them hidden? What is their resting default facial expression?

Psychological Profile: Are they introverted or extroverted? What is happiness to them? Do they have a favorite place, food, movie, etc.? Why? How do they feel about love? Being in a relationship? Are they a leader or a follower? What gets them excited? Do they have a favorite quote? What makes them angry? What are their morals? What would they do with unlimited money? Time? What is their love language? What is their Myers-Briggs type? What is their Enneagram type? What are their top 5 Clifton Strengths.

Do they have any mental disabilities?

Motivation and Fears: What do they want most in the world at the start of the story? What do they actually need most in the world? What is their biggest fear? What are they most proud of?

Family: Does your character have a family? How big is their family? Have any of them died? If so, how did this affect your central character? What is your character's current relationship with their parents? Siblings? What are some defining moments between your character and their family members?

Lifestyle: Do they enjoy their job? Do they have any other hobbies or interests? What are they competent at? Are they used to living frugally or do they enjoy a lavish lifestyle? What are their opinions towards money?

History: Where were they raised? Do they still live there? Why? What are their happiest/saddest/earliest memories? What were they like as a child? What are some of the

biggest defining moments of their life? How did they get to where they are today? What is their biggest regret? Has your character experienced any trauma?

I will often follow this prompt up by asking the AI to provide a detailed summary paragraph about who the character is, their backstory, and what motivates them the most, encouraging it to go into more detail.

Crafting Your Mini-Profile for AI Writing

After you have your enormous profile, it's time to create what I call a Mini-profile, which is an asset you will later use to prompt the AI for prose.

Let me tell you what I mean.

Later down the line, we're going to be producing scenes with AI assistance, and those scenes will obviously have characters. If you don't give the AI enough information about the characters, they are likely to come off as flat and emotionless. However, the more you give the AI about the characters, the better it will write their actions, dialogue, etc.

But if you've used the prompt above, you likely realize that it's unrealistic to include all of that information for every character in one prompt for the AI to read. While Claude could probably do it, it's easier to come up with a shorter prompt to represent each character, that gives the AI the essential details for that scene.

With that in mind, I like to end up with a single paragraph about each major character, include basic details, as well as personality types and information about how they talk. I'll explain more about this below.

For starters, if you don't know what to include, here is a prompt that you can use to summarize your character in this way:

> **Please summarize the following character profile. Be sure to include at least one sentence about what drives them, their physical description, and their mannerisms for speaking, i.e. what their dialogue sounds like. Also include their Myers-Briggs profile, Enneagram type, and Clifton Strengths.**
>
> **[INSERT CHARACTER PROFILE HERE]**

Personality Type

So, why do I use the Myers Briggs profile, Enneagram type, and Clifton Strengths in my prompts?

The key is to summarize the essence of your character in as few words as possible. This helps the AI grasp their personality quickly. I've found that most AI systems understand common personality quizzes like Myers-Briggs, Enneagram, and Clifton Strengths. You can simply state the character's types in your summary paragraph. For example:

> John is a 37-year-old detective with an ISTJ Myers-Briggs type. His Enneagram type is 1 and his top 5 Clifton Strengths are Responsibility, Focus, Harmony, Achiever, and Belief.

Providing those details gives the AI a broad sense of John's personality traits and how he might speak. That said, you may need to do some research to determine which types fit your character best. The AI won't necessarily know what's most appropriate.

Once you've assigned personality types, I recommend generating a scene with just character dialogue to see how their voices differ based on their profiles. Give the AI a prompt like:

> **Given the following character summaries, write a scene of just dialogue, nothing else.**
>
> **[INSERT CHARACTER SUMMARIES HERE]**

Reviewing the AI's dialogue scene will reveal if the personality types you've chosen manifest properly in how each character talks. Make adjustments to the profiles if needed.

Dialogue

It's important to include some brief information about how each character talks in their mini-profile. This will affect how the AI writes dialogue for that character later when you are generating scenes.

Having differentiation between character voices is key. Ideally, each character should sound unique enough that you could identify who is speaking without dialogue tags.

You can prompt the AI to include details about how a character talks in their mini-profile. However, I'd recommend reviewing and editing that information yourself. Sometimes the dialogue details the AI provides can be too generic or overly emotional. If you put too much emotion in the dialogue instructions, that character may always sound like they are experiencing that emotion.

For example, the AI might say:

> *John speaks nervously, stuttering over his words and constantly second-guessing himself.*

This is too emotional and too much of a blanket statement. If this is what you used, John would always be nervous. In reality, humans experience a wide range of emotions at any given time, and your instructions should reflect that.

Instead, focus on cadence, sentence structure, and dialogue quirks. For example:

> *John speaks slowly and deliberately, often pausing to consider his words. He has a habit of ending sentences with "you see?" when trying to make a point.*

The goal is concise, distinguishing details - not lengthy emotional descriptions. Make sure the AI focuses on word choice, cadence, dialect, and important habits more than feelings. Review the dialogue details it provides, and edit as needed to create differentiated voices for each character.

Here are a few things you can include in your prompt to make sure the sound of their dialogue is fully fleshed out:

Voice Characteristics: Establish the tone & tempo of the character, the vocabulary, diction, and educational level of speech, the pitch variation, and unique vocal patterns.

Situational Responses: How does the character respond to situations of confrontation, surprise, comfort, relaxation, or when challenged.

Relationship Dynamics: How does the character address superiors, peers, or subordinates.

Physical Tells in Scenes: What are the physical tells that the character has when feeling confident, nervous, or indifferent.

Environment and Mood Reactions: How does the character react in high-tension scenes, relaxed settings, or unknown environments?

You can run through the same exercise I used for personality types above, to make sure that the dialogue coming from your characters is believable enough.

Interact With Your Character

While optional, I really like to take everything I've developed so far, and use it to have a conversation with the character. Like I said, it's optional, but can actually be a great exercise to understand that character better.

Even if someone doesn't use AI, this can still be a fun exercise. Use a prompt like this:

Given the following character information, pretend that you are this character, and that I am someone who wants to ask you questions. Answer the questions from the perspective of the character.

[INSERT CHARACTER BIO HERE]

You'll get some fun results with that. And if you're like me, you'll likely fall down some rabbit holes.

Summary:

- Create a detailed character profile to fully understand your character before writing. This can include their background, personality, appearance, motivations, etc.

- Create a "mini-profile" for each major character - a short paragraph summing up their key traits, speaking style, and personality types like Myers-Briggs.

- Include each character's Myers-Briggs type, Enneagram type, and Clifton Strengths in their mini-profile. This quickly conveys their core personality traits to the AI.

- Include distinguishing details about how each character speaks in their mini-profile to help the AI write unique dialogue for them later. Focus on word choice, cadence, habits - not emotions.

- Optional but recommended: Have a mock conversation with your character using their profile to further understand their perspective and voice.

14

OUTLINE

Every writer has their favorite part of the writing process. Usually it's the outlining, chapter writing, editing, or even marketing.

For me? It's outlining.

And on that note: Brandon Sanderson is my personal hero. It's a dream of mine to one day collaborate with him. I've spent literal years studying his lectures, reading his books, and copying out his work by hand to try and instill it in my brain (it's a technique called copywork, look it up).

Okay yeah, I might be a bit obsessed.

But one of the things that stands out most about Brandon's process is his mastery of outlining. He's certainly not the only one who outlines, but he is the one that I've chosen to try and emulate.

So you might be surprised to know that I don't actually use AI for most of my outlining (other than to brainstorm ideas when I'm stuck).

Outlining is the one area where I genuinely revel in the manual process. It's where I find joy.

That's not to say AI doesn't have a role in my process. As I always advocate, AI should be used where you encounter the most resistance, where you find yourself staring at a blank page, unsure of where to go next. For me, that's not outlining. But for you? It might be a completely different story.

If you're someone who dreads the thought of plotting out your novel, who gets overwhelmed by the sheer number of scenes, subplots, and character arcs, then AI might just be your saving grace.

And the good news? Outlining is one of AI's biggest strengths.

Large language models thrive on structure, formulas, and patterns. As I've discussed in previous chapters on the F.I.T.S. formula, Story Hacking, and the Fractal Method, AI excels when given a framework to operate within.

So, while I might choose to do most of my outlining manually, you have the option to use AI, and I've still done a lot of study to try and get the AI outlining as well as...well, as well as Brandon Sanderson could.

I'm still working on it.

But like I said, the LLMs are great at structure, so let's look at some of the structure it already knows...

Use an Outlining Structure that the AI Knows

Most AI models have an extensive knowledge of various outlining templates. I've tested and confirmed that Claude, Gemini, and ChatGPT understand all of the following, though it does sometimes get confused, which is why it's always a good idea to already have your template mapped out before you begin outlining with it. These templates include the following:

- **The Hero's Journey:** A structure first defined by Joseph Campbell, then refined for story treatments by Christopher Vogler. It's A 12-stage narrative structure where a hero ventures from an ordinary world into a new world, faces tests and enemies, experiences a climactic ordeal, seizes a reward, resurrects to overcome a final challenge, and returns home transformed.

- **The Snowflake Method:** A planning technique created by Randy Ingermanson that starts with a one-sentence summary, expands it into one paragraph, then one page, then treatments, and finally a full draft.

- **Dan Harmon's Story Circle:** An 8-step narrative structure based on Joseph Campbell's Hero's Journey that tracks a character's journey from a zone of comfort, call to adventure, road of trials, to the climax and return home changed.

- **The Three Act Structure:** A basic story format with a beginning (Act 1), middle (Act 2), and end (Act 3) around the protagonist overcoming an obstacle to achieve a goal.

- **Save the Cat Beats:** A 15-beat narrative model popularized by Blake Snyder following story milestones like the opening image, catalyst, midpoint, and final battle.

- **The Hollywood Formula:** A basic 3-act structure focusing on a sympathetic hero overcoming odds to achieve an external goal, popularized by Syd Field.

- **Dan Wells' 7 Point Plot Structure:** A plot template mapping the hook, first plot point, first pinch point, midpoint, second pinch point, second plot point, and resolution.

- **Truby's 22 Step Structure:** John Truby's 22 key story events like weakness/need, desire, opponent, plan, battle, self-revelation.

- **James Scott Bell's LOCK System:** A 4-element approach standing for Lead character, Objective, Confrontation, and Knockout ending.

- **Freytag's Pyramid:** A 5-part dramatic structure moving from exposition, rising action, climax, falling action, and dénouement.

- **The Fichtean Curve:** A story arc based on conflict and resolution, rising to a crisis climax and descending to a dénouement.

- **The Story Spine:** A narrative formula starting with "Once upon a time" and ending "and ever since then..." hitting key points in between.

I will often start my outlining process by using a prompt like the following:

> **Using the following synopsis, create a detailed summary of the story, fleshing out additional details, and breaking it into parts using the [OUTLINE METHOD OF CHOICE]: [INSERT SYNOPSIS HERE]**

And while the AI tends to know all of the above story structure methods, it often pays to have a trusted structure of your own that you use.

Which leads me into my next point...

Bring Your Own Outlining Structure

Sometimes you have your own outlining method that you want to use, or you like to use an outlining method that the

AI doesn't know. Or even if the AI does know the structure in question, you might *still* want to bring your own adjusted or refined version of that framework to the outlining stage.

For instance, I really like the 24 Chapter Novel Outline, which was developed by Derek Murphy, and since it's presented in a chapter-by-chapter format, it works really well with AI. Here's a brief summary of that particular outline:

1. **Really Bad Day** - The protagonist is introduced facing problems in their ordinary world.

2. **Something Peculiar** - An unusual event occurs that the protagonist ignores.

3. **Grasping at Straws** - The protagonist struggles to maintain control as problems mount.

4. **Call to Adventure** - An extraordinary event forces the protagonist to abandon their goals.

5. **Head in Sand** - The protagonist tries to ignore the call to adventure.

6. **Pull Out Rug** - An event forces the protagonist into the new world against their will.

7. **Enemies & Allies** - The protagonist navigates the new world and meets characters.

8. **Games & Trials** - The protagonist faces challenges and trains in the new world.

9. **Earning Respect** - The protagonist achieves a small victory.

10. **Forces of Evil** - The protagonist encounters the antagonist's true threat.

11. **Problem Revealed** - The protagonist realizes their allies withheld information.

12. **Truth & Ultimatum** - The protagonist uncovers a big truth and must commit.

13. **Mirror Stage** - The protagonist chooses to continue despite doubts.

14. **Plan of Attack** - The protagonist devises a plan against the antagonist.

15. **Crucial Role** - The protagonist is given an important task.

16. **Direct Conflict** - The protagonist battles the antagonist's forces.

17. **Surprise Failure** - The protagonist's plan fails disastrously.

18. **Shocking Revelation** - The protagonist learns something dire about the antagonist.

19. **Giving Up** - After defeat, the protagonist loses hope.

20. **Pep Talk** - An ally encourages the protagonist.

21. **Seizing Sword** - The protagonist decides to continue despite the odds.

22. **Ultimate Defeat** - The protagonist loses the final battle.

23. **Unexpected Victory** - The protagonist prevails in an unexpected way.

24. **Bittersweet Return** - The protagonist reflects after victory.

25. **Death of Self** - The protagonist experiences rebirth. (optional)

That's a really brief summary of each chapter, but you get the idea.

Whenever I'm introducing my own structure for the AI model to use, I usually have a two-step prompt that I use that goes something like this:

> **We're going to outline a story using the following story structure. Read through the following story structure and respond by typing "..." to indicate you understand.**
>
> **[INSERT STORY FRAMEWORK HERE]**

So in the case of the 24 Chapter Novel Outline, I would insert the information about the outline beneath the prompt, then proceed to the second prompt in the sequence.

Using the above story structure, create a detailed outline using the following synopsis:

[INSERT SYNOPSIS HERE]

This now lets you expand your synopsis that you've already developed by now (hopefully) into a much more robust outline. This is why I like using the 24 chapter novel outline, because by the end of this step, I have a summary of what should happen in each individual chapter of the book.

Now, of course, you could expand those chapters, condense them, do whatever you want to them. The point is that with this method, you're able to feed the AI with any template you like, and it can use that template to convert your synopsis into an outline.

Obligatory Scenes

Another common technique that seems to work well is to ask the AI for obligatory scenes related to your genre.

For example, every individual genre and subgenre tends to have scenes that are a unique part of books in that genre, but wouldn't necessarily show up in other genres.

One of the best ways to identify these scenes is to ask the AI to identify "Obligatory Scenes" for the specified genre. Your prompt would look something like this:

Please identify [NUMBER] obligatory scenes for a [GENRE] book.

To give you an idea of what the output for this prompt looks like, here's what I got when I asked Claude to give me 20 obligatory scenes for a heist novel.

Here are 20 potential obligatory scenes for a heist novel:

1. The Planning - Where the thieves come up with the idea for the heist and start plotting how they'll pull it off.

2. Casing the Joint - Where the thieves scope out the location they plan to rob and look for potential entry points, security measures, etc.

3. Assembling the Crew - Where the thieves recruit specialists and other team members with the skills needed for the heist.

4. Staking Out the Target - Where the thieves secretly watch the location for patterns and opportunities.

5. The Prep Work - Acquiring tools, making plans, establishing alibis, etc.

6. The Dry Run - The thieves do a test run of part or all of the heist plan.

7. Raising the Stakes - Something happens to make the heist more dangerous or tempting.

8. The Point of No Return - The thieves are committed and can't back out now.

9. The Break-In - The thieves infiltrate the location.

10. Evading Security - Dodging guards, cameras, laser grids, etc.

11. Cracking the Vault - Getting into the secure area holding the loot.

12. *The Grab - Seizing the loot, whether jewelry, cash, artwork, etc.*

13. *Uh Oh! - Something goes wrong and threatens the plan.*

14. *The Chase - Getting away from security guards, police, etc pursing them.*

15. *The Great Escape - How the thieves ultimately get away with the goods.*

16. *The Aftermath - Dealing with the fallout of the heist.*

17. *Laying Low - The thieves hide out and wait for the heat to die down.*

18. *Laundering the Loot - Turning the stolen items into untraceable cash.*

19. *Splurging - Celebrating and spending their new riches.*

20. *Plotting the Next Heist - Success leads to planning an even bigger score.*

AI is great at identifying these types of scenes, though it often doesn't get all of them. So you might want to run it by a variety of chatbots, and always ask the AI if there are any more.

But overall, this is a good way to find obligatory scenes that you should *add* to your outline. These scenes could be folded into an existing scene from your general outline, but could also make an entirely new chapter.

And this is actually a lot like Brandon Sanderson's outlining method (hence why I like it so much). Brandon will outline various plot types that will make up his novel, figures out the list of scenes that are a part of that plot type, then layers them together to create a huge plot.

For example, his book Mistborn was a combination of a heist plot, a master and apprentice plot, a few character arcs that needed their own progression of scenes, and a romance plot.

Begin with the End in Mind

One last tip that I already mentioned in the Synopsis chapter, but is worth repeating here, is to begin with the end in mind.

You should already know the ending before you use the AI to outline the rest of the novel, because AI is essentially using probability to determine what it says and does. It's the same technology behind the auto-predict features on your phone. If the AI doesn't know where it's going, those words are generated randomly.

But if it knows where it's going, it can do a much better job of getting to that destination.

I and many other authors have found that by giving the AI your ending, then asking it to work backward from there to plot your novel. You'll end up with foreshadowing, additional steps that have to happen to achieve your ending, etc.

In short, it makes a much better ending, so I would always supply it with your ending (which you should hopefully have developed by now, then plot your novel from there.

Summary:

- Use story structures and outlines the AI already knows like Hero's Journey, Save the Cat, and 3-Act Structure when outlining. Give the AI the synopsis and ask it to expand using a known structure.

- Bring your own outlining structure like the 24 Chapter Novel Outline. Explain the structure to the AI in a prompt, then ask it to use that structure to outline your synopsis.

- Ask the AI to suggest common "obligatory scenes" for your genre that you can incorporate into your outline. These are scenes readers expect.

- Begin with the ending in mind. Give the AI your planned ending first, then ask it to work backwards from there, ensuring steps lead logically to the conclusion.

- The AI excels at structure so use it for outlining, but the author may prefer to manually outline too for creative enjoyment. Use AI where you get stuck.

15

Story Beats

Story Beats are the last step before you begin actually writing the prose of your book. Even if you are using the discovery writing methods I outlined in an earlier chapter, you are likely using some form of story beat as your prompt for the next block of text that the AI gives you.

I'm going to give you two possible prompts to use here. The first is a simple starter prompt, while the second is more complex. Which you choose to use will depend on your goals.

The Starter Story Beat Prompt

By now, you should have a completed outline with at least a sentence or two (if not a fully fleshed-out paragraph) for each chapter. To create the story beats, I will often start with this starter prompt that you will repeat for each chapter of your outline. It looks something like this:

Take the following chapter summary, and generate a list of 12 highly detailed action beats with additional story information to fully flesh out the chapter and prepare it for a ghostwriter to write. Make sure to always use proper nouns instead of pronouns.

Note: You can replace "12" with any number you want. I find that between 12-20 is usually sufficient.

This will flesh out that single chapter summary into a detailed list of what actually happens in that chapter. Think of it as an even more detailed outline.

The bit about using proper nouns is also very intentional. Because you will want your story beats to be very clear on who is doing what. If you're constantly using pronouns, the AI may get confused about who you are talking about when you are generating prose, so it's important that you're using names whenever possible.

As always, be specific.

The Structure of a Scene

As I was researching these prompts, I realized that most AI authors were just asking the AI for beats and leaving it at that. But what I began to understand, was that every scene can and should have structure. It's a microcosm of a story, a small standalone story of its own, with a beginning, middle, and climax.

Unfortunately, there is no one-size-fits-all model for every scene. It will depend on many factors, such as does the scene take place at the beginning or end of the novel? Is it a proactive or reactive scene? Does it involve internal or external conflict, or both?

That said, there are a few common elements in a scene, which I have included in this two-part prompt to get even more specific results out of the AI when you prompt it. Here is the prompt:

> **Take the following chapter summary, and generate additional STORY INFORMATION to fully flesh out the scene.**
>
> **Chapter Summary: [INSERT YOUR CHAPTER SUMMARY HERE]**
>
> **Included information on the following:**
>
> **POV: Who is the point of view character for the scene?**
>
> **Setting: Establish where this scene takes place. If appropriate, include some kind of external conflict generated by the setting.**

Examples could include (but are not limited to) changes in weather, proximity to another source of conflict or tension, a place of negative significance to one or more of the characters, etc.

First Line: What is a good first line that hooks the reader? A good example would be something action-oriented, or a line of dialogue.

Turning point: What is the turning point, or inciting incident that puts the character(s) in a new situation, upsetting the status quo and beginning the scene's momentum? This can be something going wrong, a complication, a conflict between characters, or even something going really well. This doesn't have to be a big thing, but can be subtle, like a simple change in attitude, or a decision being made. This should take place early in the scene.

Conflict: What is the driving internal and external conflict of the scene? How does this conflict create tension and enhance the pacing of the scene? How does it increase the rising action of the scene?

Character Change: How does this scene change the viewpoint character for better or worse? What choice(s) does the character make, whether internal, external, subtle, or important?

Climax: What is the climax of the scene, and how does it affect the character(s)? How does it show the consequences of the character's choices?

Reaction: After the climax, how does the character(s) react to the climax?

Cliffhanger: What is the final line of the scene, and how does it set up a cliffhanger ending leading to the following scene?

Then, once it has given you all of that information, you can edit it how you like, and use this prompt to generate your beats?

Given the following information, give me a list of 12 highly detailed action beats with additional STORY INFORMATION to fully

flesh out the chapter. Make sure to always use proper nouns instead of pronouns.

[INSERT YOUR EDITED INFORMATION FROM PREVIOUS PROMPT HERE]

Validate Your Story Beats

Now, many of you are not going to want to use the longer prompt, as it does involve extra steps. But it does force you to think through some of these important aspects of a scene that you'll want to consider.

After all, you want to make sure that the scene has no boring bits. A good scene structure is one way to help with this.

That said, I personally don't use these prompts too often, except as a way to generate ideas for myself. That's because I personally love the process of writing these beats out myself. It's one of my favorite parts of writing.

So I just write the beats out manually, one at a time.

But regardless of whether you use these prompts or not, there is one thing you need to do at this stage, and that is to validate your beats.

This is something you should have been doing all along this process, editing your synopsis, outline, characters, etc, to be exactly the story you want to write. But it is especially important that you do so here.

The reason for this is that the next step is writing the actual prose. And the quality of that prose will depend *significantly* on the specificity of your beats.

If you want it included in your final manuscript, it needs to be included in your beats.

That's why I tend to write most of them myself, or *heavily* edit the beats that the AI gives me. Because I know what makes a good scene better than the AI does. I am also the continuity director. I know the backstory of the character, I know where the story is going, and what a character would or wouldn't do in a given situation. These are facts that the AI doesn't know (or if it does, it is likely to misuse or misrepresent).

So spend the time to make these beats shine. It will result in a much better book on the backend.

Summary:

- Story beats are a detailed outline of what happens in each chapter. They come after the overall story outline is done.

- You can use a simple starter prompt asking the AI to generate several highly detailed beats per chapter. Specify using proper nouns, not pronouns.

- Alternatively, use a more complex 2-part prompt that ensures each scene has good structure - establishing the POV, setting, hook, conflict, turning point, climax, reaction and cliffhanger.

- Regardless of the method you use to generate beats, validate and edit them to ensure they align to your vision before generating prose. Beats dictate prose quality.

- Be highly specific in beats. Include anything you want represented in the final manuscript.

- Invest time in making beats great, as this directly translates to better prose. Beats are the final step before writing.

16

DEVELOPING YOUR STYLE

Before we dive deeper into the craft of writing compelling fiction, I have one last VERY important step for you: how to develop an effective style prompt.

When I first started out writing with AI, I was using Sudowrite to generate my initial drafts. And the results...weren't great.

At first, I was discouraged by the mushy, unrealistic prose it produced. The dialogue was cheesy, the characters interacted in chummy-chummy, unrealistic ways, and the descriptions were overwrought. As a result, my draft chapters required *extensive* editing before they were ready for readers.

But then I realized the power of the style prompt.

By carefully crafting a prompt that gave Sudowrite very specific instructions, I found I could dramatically cut down on the editing required. Style is arguably the most important part of your AI writing prompt, next to the story beats covered in the last chapter.

As you practice writing with ChatGPT, Claude, or Sudowrite, you should constantly tweak and update your style prompt to refine it. This will result in much cleaner initial drafts that require far less editing. It will also give you more consistent tones between chapters.

Let's look at some types of effective style prompts.

Types of Style Prompts:

There are basically three ways to structure your style prompts, depending on which program you're using: short, long, and very long.

Short Style Prompts

This one is primarily for working in Sudowrite, although you can use short style prompts in any program. But in Sudowrite, your style prompt needs to be 40 words or less due to character limitations. Here is an example of a short style prompt I have used successfully:

> "First person past point of view of [main character], show don't tell, deep point of view. Realistic dialogue. Stronger verbs. Lots of conflict, drama, and description. Avoid mushy descriptions/dialogue."

This gives the AI clear, concise instructions to write in an engaging, vivid style while avoiding the pitfalls of unrealistic, overly flowery prose. Adjust the details to match the tone and style you are aiming for.

Longer Style Prompts:

If you are using a tool like Novelcrafter, you are free to include much more complicated prompts, potentially in the hundreds of words (although that might end up being too bloated, which also can disrupt the quality of the output).

For instance, you could take each part of the shorter style prompt above (show don't tell, realistic dialogue, etc.), and give more detailed explanations and examples of what the style should look like.

Feel free to really go to town on your longer style prompts. Anytime you see an AI acting in a way you don't like, simply ask it not to do that thing, or give it more positive examples of what it should look like.

I've literally had so many authors come up to me and ask: How do I get ChatGPT to stop doing __?

The answer is pretty simple: ask it not to do that thing. Or better yet, figure out what it should be doing instead, and ask it to do that (AI deals with positives better than negatives).

Really Long Style Prompts

If you are using Claude, you can have VERY long style prompts. I like to take what I have in the longer style prompt above, but then add a sample chapter or two to give the AI an example of the prose style that I'm looking for.

I'll talk about the "Super Prompt" later in the next chapter, but that will often include an example chapter with a little instruction. Here's what I use:

> **The following is a sample chapter of my writing. Do not use any story information from this chapter, but analyze it only for the prose style.**

This ensures that the AI isn't actually using the prose of the chapter for story guidance, although you can mitigate this issue if you use the previous chapter in the book, in which case you could tweak the above instructions to let it know that you're using the previous chapter.

Analyze Your Writing

One of the desires I hear most from authors is the ability to get the AI writing in their own specific style. Personally, I think it won't be long before it will be easy to create our own, fine-tuned models that mimick our voice well, but in the meantime, there are a couple of strategies to use:

First, if you are using Claude, you can literally plop a sample chapter or two into your prompt, and ask it to write in that style. This is one of the best ways to do this.

However, this isn't possible everywhere (for now), so here is the other method:

Please a sample of your writing into the chatbot (Sudowrite has a feature for this as well), and ask it to analyze your work for style and tone. The AI should respond with a bunch of things that the writing does well, or other specific quirks to the style.

Now this feedback isn't perfect. It's not even always accurate, so you'll want to take what it gives you with a grain of salt. However, you can cherry pick a lot of style prompts and examples from the results that the AI gives you, and use that to craft your style prompt.

I've got a list of potential style prompts below, some of which I obtained with this method. However, you will want to review them carefully, and make sure to test everything out, and tweak as you go.

Using Someone Else's Style

There's another method that many use, which is to ask the AI to write in the style of a particular author.

The reason I didn't talk about this first, is because I personally believe this is an ethical gray area. Some AI authors disagree with me on this, and there is certainly nothing illegal about using an existing author's style (you can't copyright a style under U.S. law). But I personally draw the line at using an author's style for work that I intend to publish and make money on.

That said, there are more ethical ways to do it, including the following:

For Experimentation Only

Sometimes it helps to use an author's style just as an experiment. Let's say you test a style prompt on your work, then you ask it to rewrite it in the style of a particular author. Then, notice what it does differently, and maybe try again with the style of a different author to note the difference.

Not only is this a fun exercise, but you will actually learn a lot about what sets that author apart in their tone.

Use Public Domain Authors

Let's say you're writing a regency romance book, or perhaps a 19th century detective novel. Using the styles of Jane Austen or Sir Arthur Conan Doyle, respectively, is a great way to add some additional authenticity to your novel that you might not have been able to do on your own. And if the style is too much, you could tweak your style prompt to be just for dialogue, or only use it in key moments.

Public domain authors are plentiful, and while they tend to be older styles, and not always perfect for the style you're looking for, it's a treasure trove of possibility.

Analyze an Author's Style

One thing you can do is analyze the style of an existing author, much in the same way that you would analyze your own work in the technique I mentioned above. But since most famous and prolific authors have likely been used to train the algorithm, you can usually just ask the AI what it knows about the prose style of that author.

Notice, I said "prose style". If you ask to analyze an author's style, it will likely tell you about larger, big-picture things about that style. For example, when I ask it about Brandon Sanderson's style, it tends to mention things like his complex magic systems, worldbuilding, and unique twists. When I ask it for the prose style, it gives me better results that are more appropriate.

Once I have a list of things I've learned about the prose style of a particular author, I can then include those things in the style prompt.

Suggested Style Options to Experiment With

So I've explained a lot of what I've mentioned so far to many different authors, and I often get the same response: okay,

Jason, that's fine and all, but what are some *actual* prompts I should consider using in my style prompt?

First of all, do not skip the steps above, and don't skip experimentation, because its testing and iterating on a prompt that will ultimately result in the best output.

Additionally, it will also depend a LOT on what model you're using, because one style prompt might yield completely different results with a different model.

That said, here are a few elements of a style prompt that you should at least consider and test.

- Point of view (first person, third person limited, third person omniscient, etc.)

- Viewpoint character (make sure to specify who we are seeing the events of the chapter through)

- Tense (past, present, etc.)

- Fast-paced action and snappy dialogue

- Grounded realism

- Tight, punchy sentences and descriptive language

- Quick dialogue with short quips and comebacks

- Let the dialogue and action explain the story (show, don't tell)

- Varied sentence structure and length: Use a mix of

short and long sentences, as well as different sentence structures, to create a more engaging and dynamic flow of words

- Make the dialogue sound real with common human quirks: craft dialogue that reflects natural speech patterns, but don't overdo slang or sayings.

- Use pacing that fits the scene: Use quick, short sentences and paragraphs for exciting or action-filled parts and longer sentences for slower, more introspective scenes.

- Maintain a consistent tone: make the tone of the writing consistent throughout the paragraphs, avoiding sudden shifts in formality or style.

- Intelligently shuffle and rephrase the text: Alter the sentence structure, introduce synonyms or paraphrase and adjust the arrangement of words and phrases in a sentence, as well as the relationships between them, to create subtle variations in the structure of the text.

- Avoid using the following words: that, feel/feeling/felt, back, just, then, all, look, maybe, knew/know.

- Use strong verbs: Choose powerful action words instead of using adverbs.

- Use euphonic words, onomatopoeia, and strong similes: Bring more life to the prose with these but use them sparingly throughout the text.

Summary:

- Develop an effective style prompt to improve your AI-generated drafts. Constantly tweak and update it as you go.

- Longer style prompts in chatbots can be more detailed. Explain and give examples.

- Claude allows very long style prompts with sample chapters. Ask it to mimic that style.

- Analyze your own writing or an author's to identify elements to include in your prompt.

- Use public domain authors' styles if appropriate. Analyze famous styles, but focus on prose.

- Test point of view, tense, pacing, realism, sentence length, dialogue, consistency in tone.

- Keep iterating. The key is constant testing and refining your style prompt.

17

THE PROSE

I t's time.

Time for the final step in the process: writing the prose with AI.

By now, you should understand that it's impossible to write good prose without a LOT of preparation, basically all of the chapters we've covered so far.

And you might not even want AI for this process, and that's fine. Many authors only use AI for 1-2 steps in this process (often brainstorming).

But for those who want to go all the way and use the AI for writing prose, read on.

And I have good news.

If you've done all of the steps in the process so far, writing prose is relatively easy. In fact, assuming you have story beats for your entire novel already, you could (in theory) generate the entire book in a single day.

This is how you do it....

The Superprompt

So far, I've found that the concept of the superprompt is the best way to write prose for fiction. However, the exact strategy you use will be slightly different depending on which AI model or software you are using. For example, both Novelcrafter and Sudowrite are essentially crafting their own superprompt on the backend by assembling all of the different elements of your story so far (the beats, the character information, etc.) and crafting a long superprompt that they submit to the AI on their end, which then spits out a result.

However, if you've got a chatbot with a large enough context window (which most of them have), you could do this superprompt right in a chatbot or API playground.

But I'm teaching this to you so you can understand this: that most AI software are just using the same AI models that you are, but crafting their own superprompt using very similar techniques to what you see below, in order to simplify the process for their users.

By understanding the concepts behind the superprompt, you'll be able to look at what these tools are doing and (if they allow it) potentially tweak or improve on the default prompts that they use. This is something I do all the time in Novelcrafter, for example.

This is what the skeleton of the superprompt looks like:

<instructions>
</instructions>

<sample chapter>
</sample chapter>

<characters>
</characters>

<setting>
</setting>

<outline>
</outline>

<chapter beats>
</chapter beats>

```
<style>
</style>
```

We use the <>, </> format because this is a structure often used in coding. I'm not a coder, but I do know HTML. In HTML, we distinguish between different objects by the same technique. For example, if you wanted to have bolded text, you would use the following HTML markup: <strong>Your bolded text here</strong>.

Many AI documentation actually *recommends* prompting their LLM in this way.

So in essence, using this type of markup clearly indicates to the AI when a specific section begins and when it ends, so it doesn't get confused. It's like taking all of the material that we've gathered so far, and organizing it into neat little boxes for easy retrieval.

So let's talk about what we put in each of these sections:

<sample chapter>

This is a section that I typically only use when writing in a model with large context windows like Claude.

Giving the AI a sample chapter makes it easy for it to learn from and mimic your style. I will usually include a prompt like the following before I paste in my sample chapter:

The following is a sample chapter of my writing. Do not use any story information from this chapter, but analyze it only for the prose style. We will be using this prose style in <instructions>.

Then I simply copy/paste my sample chapter below, and finish off with the </sample chapter> tag after.

<characters>

Next, I like to show the AI my characters. In most cases, you will definitely need to use the shorter description that I talk about in the characters chapter. At a minimum, I like to include a brief physical description, their personality types, and how they typically react in certain types of situations.

With Claude, you can afford to paste a more detailed character profile. Feel free to do this, especially with the more important characters.

Then finish off with the </characters> tag.

<setting>

This is where you put information on the setting for the scene you are about to write. This will change from one scene to the next, so be sure to update this part with each new generation.

This is also where you can put any pertinent worldbuilding or research that you'd like the AI to know for the scene. However, I don't recommend you include all of your worldbuilding/research unless it is relevant to the scene in question, because otherwise the AI might pull in details that aren't necessary. This also lets you keep the word count down.

Then finish off with the </setting> tag.

<outline>

For the outline, I like to put the entire outline for the entire novel in this space, but that can often lead to a prompt that is too big for some tools like ChatGPT, so you can theoretically leave this part out, or only include the summary of the scene you are about to write.

Then finish off with the </outline> tag.

<chapter beats>

The Chapter Beats section is one of the most important, it's where you put all of the detailed chapter beats that you've developed so far.

I've found that with Claude, I'm able to put all of the beats in one superprompt to generate the entire chapter at once. With ChatGPT, I've struggled to get that kind of output, so often I will limit the number of beats I use in the super-prompt to 2-3, then do the next 2-3, etc. etc.

Then finish off with the </chapter beats> tag.

<style>

This is where you put your style that we developed in the previous chapter. This is in addition to the sample chapter that you may or may not have also included. This is also where I would put a few key details, such as the point of view and tense.

Then finish off with the </style> tag.

<instructions>

Finally, we have the instructions, where we tell the AI what you want it to do with all of this information. Here is a sample of an instructions prompt that I have used before:

> **Using all of the information on <chapter beats>, <outline>, <setting>, and <characters>, write 5,000 words of chapter 1. Use the <sample chapter> and the <style> to determine the prose style of the output. Follow the <chapter beats> closely. All paragraphs should take place during the timeframe of the summary instead of adding**

new events. Focus on fully developing the given story beats rather than rushing to new plot points. End the scenes at the specified story beat rather than continuing further.

Notice that I said 5,000 words. As of this writing, this seems to be a good way to get some of the LLMs to write longer text responses. I've seen as many as 3000 words in one prompt. It's not 5,000 words, obviously, but giving it a large number like that causes Claude to stretch. Otherwise the average is much lower, i.e. 400-600 words at a time.

If I were modifying this prompt to only include the next 500-600 words instead of a full chapter, I would do something like this:

Using all of the information on <chapter beats>, <outline>, <setting>, and <characters>, write 900 words of a chapter. Use the <sample chapter> and the <style> to determine the prose style of the output. Follow the <chapter beats> closely. All paragraphs should take place during the timeframe of the summary instead of adding new events. Focus on fully developing the given story beats rather than rushing to new plot

points. End the scenes at the specified story beat rather than continuing further.

While I still give it a large number of words, in this case 900, I'm still not expecting it to get that far. Usually I can expect 500-600 words from that kind of a prompt, depending on the model I'm using. So be prepared to not generate the entire chapter at once. Just work 2-3 story beats at a time, then continue with the next 2-3, and run the prompt again.

Finish off this section with the </instructions> tag.

Rinse and Repeat

Once you've got your superprompt constructed, which shouldn't take long if you've done all of the other steps, it's a simple matter of running the prompt over and over again, and swapping out the important bits as you go.

Here are some of the things you may have to swap out:

- **Sample Chapter:** You can potentially leave this the same, but it can sometimes help to change it to the previous chapter that you generated. Just make sure the previous chapter is fully edited to be exactly how you would like it.

- **Characters:** Make sure you only use the characters that are relevant to the scene.

- **Setting:** Make sure the setting matches the current

scene.

- **Chapter Beats:** Obviously, the chapter beats should be different for each chapter.

- **Other tweaks:** I would briefly scan through the entire prompt to make sure there aren't any other bits you will need to tweak (like the chapter number in the <instructions>, for example).

And then you simply rinse and repeat until you have generated all of the chapters. I like to use Novelcrafter because it makes this process much easier, automatically pulling in the sample chapter, style, setting, characters, etc. and lets me focus entirely on writing the beats for the scene and then editing the output from those beats.

I Recommend One Section at a Time

While you can generate all of your chapters rapidly, without looking at them closely, I would advise against this until you are experienced with generating prose with AI.

The reason is two-fold:

1. You will likely realize that your beats or style prompt need adjustment to improve your output. If you take the time to edit each chapter that you just generated, identify what the AI could improve, then tweak your style prompt, you are likely to get better and

better results with each chapter.

2. You may find that the AI falls off the tracks now and again. I've tried to include sample prompts that keep the AI focused on your instructions, but I almost always get the AI trying to continue the story after my story beats, which just have to be cut out with the edit. But in some cases, you may find that it got distracted and didn't follow your instructions well enough. If so, you may need to try again.

So while you can generate all your chapters in a day (assuming you have all your story information ready to go), I would advise you to generate one chapter, edit it how you like, adjust your prompt, then move on to the next chapter.

Summary:

- The Superprompt is the best way to write prose with AI. It can contain sections for a Sample Chapter, Characters, Setting, Outline, Chapter Beats, Style, and Instructions.

- The Sample Chapter allows the AI to mimic your writing style. Use a full chapter sample with Claude

- Characters section has brief descriptions of relevant characters. Keep it short for ChatGPT.

- Setting has details on the setting for the specific scene. Include only relevant worldbuilding.

- Outline contains the full outline or just the scene summary. Helpful for context.

- Chapter Beats has the detailed beats for the scene. Just use 2-3 at a time for ChatGPT.

- Style sets the prose style, POV, tense, etc.

- Instructions tell the AI exactly what to write. Specify word count. Update beats and settings each time.

- Generate and edit one chapter at a time before moving to the next. This allows you to tweak the style prompt and beats to improve quality.

18

EDITING

By now, we've essentially completed the Fractal process for writing a book with AI, but your book is far from complete.

Now, it's time to edit.

Some people hate editing, but I will tell you right now, you are going to need to heavily edit these words. It's one of the prices you pay for writing prose as effortlessly as we do with AI.

Now if you've written the prose yourself, you don't have to worry about it as much. Not more than you would normally do, anyway.

But if you're writing with AI, you're going to need at least one additional edit pass to what you would normally do. This first pass looks for unique issues that are common to AI.

Personally, I edit each chapter right after I've finished generating it, and *before* I move on to the next chapter. Though I know some who will generate all of the chapters first. I only recommend this if you're already a seasoned AI pro, and feel confident enough in your prompting to not need frequent prompt-tweaking or reiteration.

Editing the AI Output

Here are some of the problems common with AI writing that you will want to look for:

- **Inconsistencies:** Often the world, setting, characters, descriptions, etc. will contain inconsistencies from chapter to chapter, since the AI doesn't think in terms of "hey, I said that architecture was gothic in the last chapter but in this chapter it's Romanesque". Remember, you are the continuity director. You need to keep it on track.

- **Redundancies:** Often you will find the AI saying the same thing over and over again. This could be with a particular turn of phrase, but often happens with certain details, such as a character's physical description. You can adjust the prompt by taking those things out of the character description, adding certain words or phrases to your "Avoid" list in your style prompt, etc. Thankfully, these are easy to edit out as long as you spot them.

- **Flowery language:** Most language models (but especially the GPT models) tend to get a little over the top, flowery, and melo-dramatic. This is one of the most important reasons for a solid style prompt, because without it you will be spending most of your time cutting back and rewriting this type of language. *With* a good style prompt, the output will get significantly better, though it's almost never perfect. Plan to spend some time cutting flowery prose.

- **Sidetracked AI:** It's common for pretty much every model to get sidetracked and for the AI to take your story in a different direction, especially after it gets to the end of your beats. These models tend to like to tie up the stories in a nice little bow, and will often steer the story in this way. This is the biggest thing to watch out for, because sometimes you won't realize it's happening until much later. If you're lucky, all you will have to do is just chop off the last few paragraphs from the output. If you're not, you may find the entire chapter went completely off the rails and needs to be rewritten/regenerated.

This is why I recommend reading through each chapter/section right after you've generated it. You can check for all of these things, adjust your prompt if needed, and either try again or move on to the next chapter with an improved prompt. The better your prompt (especially the style), the less editing you will need to do at the end.

I know some authors who don't keep 90% of what the AI gives them for prose. They just rewrite most of it, and that's okay. AI is sometimes best used as a way to get past writers block. Many authors want to continue doing most of the writing themselves, and when you have generated prose with AI, it can often clue you in on where the story should go, so you can focus just on writing the prose yourself, and not having to think about where the chapter should be going.

But all that said, one of the common questions I get is about editing *with* AI, not just editing AI output. Are there tools and techniques that are useful for editing with AI?

Editing *With* AI

So, personally, I don't really like to use AI for editing. Yes, it can sometimes accurately catch a few typos or awkward sentences, or it can improve the readability of certain passages. However, I find it rather awkward due to the clumsiness of putting all of the prose into the chatbot in small chunks and asking it for consistent results.

Plus, sometimes I find the suggestions Claude/ChatGPT give are too generic and not really helpful. It's as though it's just telling you what one might *expect* to hear in your feedback, and not actual feedback you can/should take action on.

So all in all, I feel like proper editing requires human judgement for the entire process.

However.

There are two tools that I do recommend for editing: AutoCrit and ProWritingAid.

AutoCrit is a tool that flags various common issues that you are likely to find in a given book, things like cliche phrases, overused dialogue tags besides said/asked, overuse of adverbs, etc.

A lot of these things that AutoCrit flags are things that AI has difficulty with, meaning it serves as a great tool to find the areas where the AI is being a bit too AI-ish, and edit those out with your human input.

Additionally, AutoCrit has some great comparison tools that allow you to compare your book to other books in the genre. Perhaps your adverbs are no better/worse than other books in the same genre, so you don't have to edit as many of them out. It's a great way to get peace of mind that your book will fit in the genre.

ProWritingAid is different. It's a proofreading tool that uses AI to scan for specific problems with your writing, be they spelling/grammar issues, run-on sentences, awkward phrases, adverbs, passive voice. You name it, they've got a report for it. It's similar to AutoCrit, but more specialized in the spelling/grammar side of things.

Both are great tools to help with your editing, and I would recommend a combination of both of them, together with your own human intuition, over tools like ChatGPT or Claude for editing.

Summary:

- The AI output will likely need heavy editing to fix inconsistencies, redundancies, flowery language, and sidetracked storylines. Read through each chapter after generating.

- Don't rely solely on AI tools like Claude or ChatGPT for editing, as they lack human judgment.

- Consider using AutoCrit's tools to identify common issues that AI frequently makes in its prose.

- Use ProWritingAid to scan for issues like grammar, awkward phrasing, passive voice, etc.

- Editing is still best done by humans, but AI tools like AutoCrit and ProWritingAid can assist with certain tasks more easily than writing from scratch.

Part III

Alternative Methods

Myth HQ, LLC

19

DIALOGUE FIRST APPROACH

While the fractal technique that I have now walked you through is (I believe) the best way to write quickly with AI, I would be remiss if I didn't mention some other tactics. Because my method is just one way to do things, and there are plenty of others (this is why I recommend everyone should experiment).

One of these other tactics is somewhat similar to my approach, but instead of story beats, we generate dialogue.

Think of this as creating the skeleton of a story, then using AI to flesh out the details.

(By the way, huge shout out to my friend Mendi, for helping me with some of these prompts.)

So, for most of the process you could still follow the steps of the Fractal Method, but with a couple of key differences. Here are a few:

Additional Time Spent Crafting Speech Styles

If you're taking a dialogue first approach, you'll want to focus more on the dialogue style. There are plenty of prompts to get improved style of your dialogue (I listed several in the style chapter), as well as to get unique character voices (see my characters chapter).

But here are a few other areas where you could include with your characters to get more distinct dialogue:

- **Subconscious:** give examples of the inner dialogue that a character might or might not have.

- **Words/Cadence:** list the kind of words, speech patters, education level, etc. that the character commonly uses.

- **Body language:** What kind of body language does the character have? This will influence dialogue as well.

- **Pacing/interaction:** How does the character interact with different groups of people? How do they react while in situations of stress, calm, conflict, etc.

Once you have tightly-crafted characters and character voices, you can move on to the dialogue-first draft.

Dialogue-First Draft

Now, the amount of information that you give the AI can vary. In fact, while I said you can skip the story beats section, you might even want to keep it to get that specific story detail.

If you do end up keeping the story beats, it means that you're adding an additional step to the overall process, but the quality is likely to be better with the specific story detail found in the beats.

So whatever you decide to do, here is the prompt I would lead with:

> **Using the following story summary, write in a DIALOGUE DRAFT format for an award-winning TV script. Avoid unnecessary dialogue.**

The AI will then create an entire script out of the story beats, usually with mostly dialogue and minimal exposition.

The next step will be to take the output, edit it as needed, and then it's time to feed it back into the AI to get all of the other "stuff" that comes around the dialogue. Your prompt might look something like this:

> **Transform this dialogue draft script into prose suitable for a bestselling [GENRE] novel. KEEP THE DIALOGUE VERBATIM. ONLY USE ACTION BEATS TO ATTRIBUTE DIALOGUE and OMIT EVERY SPEECH TAG. Add vivid, visceral descriptions. Add im-

mersive action beats that reveal character movements, emotions, and mood. Prioritize showing over telling.

Now, you can easily get more complicated than this and really optimize these prompts, but I just wanted to give you a general overview of how it works. Overall, not much changes in the Fractal Approach other than adding this additional step.

So why might you want to use this method instead of the "normal" approach? After all, this adds an extra step, which means more time.

Well, first of all, there's a whole group of authors who actually write this way: developing the dialogue first, then filling in the details. It's a great way to write.

(Another shout out to my friend Jeff Elkins and his book: *The Dialogue Doctor Will See You Now: How to Write Dialogue and Characters Readers will Love*)

Second, dialogue is often one of those things that the AI struggles with. It often enters "uncanny valley" territory, because a part of our brain realizes that people don't necessarily talk that way. So if you can draw attention to this, and fix up the dialogue before doing any of the rest of the work, it lets you prioritize this highly-important area in a way that improves the overall writing with minimal effort (since all you have to worry about is writing the dialogue).

AI is great at writing description and expository information (i.e. everything around the dialogue). So if you can get the dialogue straight, it should have no problem filling in the rest.

Summary:

- An alternative/addition to the fractal method is to focus on crafting dialogue first before generating prose.

- Spend extra time refining character voices and dialogue styles. Add details like inner dialogue, word choice, body language.

- Generate a dialogue-only draft from your story summary. Edit as needed.

- Feed the edited dialogue back into the AI to add description, action, etc. around the existing dialogue.

- This puts extra focus on improving a challenging area (dialogue). The AI can more easily fill in narrative elements around solid dialogue.

20

Tips For the Discovery Writer

One of the questions I get asked the most is, "how can I use AI as a discovery writer."

(Often the word is "pantser", meaning those that write by the seat of their pants, but I'll be using the softer term.)

I actually struggled with this question for a long time, before I eventually found some answers.

The reason, I'm not a discovery writer. I am a heavy outliner.

And honestly, it really does seem (to me) that AI caters to outliners a little better, mostly because it responds well to frameworks, and outlines are a classic example of a framework in fiction. And indeed, most of this book is really structured more for outliners than discovery writers (although the latter can still make use of much of it).

However, I eventually talked to a friend of mine, Steph, who is a discovery writer and uses AI all the time. She's also the founder of Facebook's biggest community of AI Writers, which you should definitely check out. It's called AI Writing for Authors.

Anyway, Steph pointed me to a few techniques that are really helpful if you use AI as a discovery writer. Plus, I've added a few of my own that I've learned as discovery-writing techniques in other contexts.

I also recommend checking out J. Thorn's book, Discovery Writing with ChatGPT: AI-Powered Storytelling, where he documents his journey discovery writing a brilliant piece of experimental fiction, one that is actually told through chat, and it's so cool! It's the perfect example of how we can get *new* forms of storytelling that couldn't have existed without AI.

But I digress.

Here are some of the methods I would use if I were a discovery writer:

You Can Still Brainstorm

Even as a discovery writer, brainstorming can be an invaluable first step before diving into your story. AI tools like ChatGPT or Claude are great for generating ideas, character profiles, settings, plot points, and more to get your creative juices flowing.

Every writer is on a kind of spectrum. It's not just outliners on one side, and discovery writers on the other. For example, my friend Steph still likes to have an idea of where the story is going, but generally allows for a lot of creative freedom on how to get there.

Regardless, there will come a time when you need some information that you simply don't have on hand, or would take you a while to dream up. That's where the AI will come in handy.

Start by asking your AI assistant broad, open-ended questions about your story premise. For example, **"Can you give me 10 interesting character traits for the main character in my romance novel set in 1920s Paris?"** Review the list it provides, picking the traits that resonate and inspire you most. Ask follow-up questions to expand on those ideas.

You can also use your AI assistant to brainstorm obstacles, conflicts, and events that could unfold in your story. Give it your core premise, time period, location, and main characters. Then ask it to generate a list of major plot points or scenes that could happen. See if any intrigue you or spark new directions to explore as you begin writing.

Don't feel locked in by any of the AI's ideas, especially if you're a discovery writer. Brainstorming is meant to give you jumping off points, not a pre-determined story structure. Let the possibilities marinate as you begin discovery writing. Follow where your characters and story want to take you organically. You might end up using some of the AI's suggestions, putting your own spin on them, or disregarding them entirely. The key is flexibly.

Edit as You Go, One Beat at a Time

Discovery writing means letting the story unfold as you write your first draft, without an extensive outline planned ahead of time. But that doesn't mean you can't edit and refine a bit as you go. Using your AI assistant in focused bursts for editing can tighten your writing and clarify the emerging story beat by beat.

Rather than starting with an outline, try feeding the AI one story beat at a time. You can then take the output it gives you, fix it up to your liking, feed it back into the AI with a prompt like **"Here is my revised version of what you wrote. Now continue the story with..."** and provide it with the next beat.

This is the most common way that discovery writers use AI in their writing, bit by bit. It's a slightly slower process than what an outliner might use with AI, but it's still effective, and still much faster than typing it out on your own.

Bear in mind that a lot of the principles found in this book still apply to discovery writing. This is especially true of things like getting your style prompts correct.

And indeed, discovery writers might actually have a slight advantage, because going through this process of feeding the AI little chunks of your edited words, it will learn your style from the examples, and be able to emulate it better in future output.

Yes, but... No, and...

This is a framework that I learned from Mary Robinette Kowal (via Brandon Sanderson's college course) about a handy technique to use when discovery writing.

It's a good way to keep the tension heightened, and forces the plot to stay interesting.

It's called "Yes, but... No, and..."

Basically, your character is trying to do something in every scene (or at least they should be). So with every attempt to solve their problem, that character should either succeed or fail. The concept behind this is to ask yourself at the end of each scene (or even multiple times throughout the scene) if they succeeded at the thing they were trying to do.

If the answer is yes, you should add a "but", a complication that happened even though the protagonist succeeded, thus keeping the conflict going. If the answer is no, you add an "and" to show that even more conflict is piling on top of the character.

There are two ways you can use the AI to make use of this awesome framework:

1. **Ask the AI to Choose:** Once the AI has written a section of a scene for you, ask the AI if the character has succeeded in their objective, then instruct it to use the "Yes, but... No, and..." solution with a prompt like, **"For the next part of the scene, use a "Yes, but... No, and..." framework to determine what**

happens next. Did the character obtain [her/her] objective? If yes, say "Yes, but…" and point out a potential complication or conflict. If no, say "No, and" and specify what else might have happened instead to further increase the conflict and tension. Do not write the scene yet, and instead present me with your solution for my approval."

2. **Have the AI Ask You:** For each scene you write, instruct the AI to ask you what happens next using this framework with a prompt like this. "When you finish writing this scene, ask me for what comes next by asking me if the character has obtained their objective yet." And then you simply give it your own answer when it finishes the scene with a "Yes, but… No, and…"

Tips for Discovery Writing in Novelcrafter or Sudowrite

Now, everything I've talked about so far is using a chatbot interface like what we have in ChatGPT or Claude. But for many authors, you might be using another program.

And the biggest two, as of this writing, are Novelcrafter and Sudowrite, both of which are designed for fiction writing.

Both of these programs allow you to enter in information about your characters, settings, outline, etc. but neither one makes it obligatory to prepare all of that information ahead of time.

For instance, when you get ready to start a chapter, think of the location where this new scene is based, and write a little information about it. Enter that as a "Codex" entry in Novelcrafter or a Worldbuilding element in Sudowrite. Then make sure that information is known to the AI as you write the next beat.

Then, instead of writing all the story beats out ahead of time, simply write them out one at a time, and running those beats through Novelcrafter/Sudowrite's respective writing tools. No need to have the whole outline prepared ahead of time.

What Would I Do?

I've already mentioned that I'm not really a discovery writer. I like my outlines too much.

But because I'm also a fan of experimenting, I probably will discovery write a book at some point. When I do, this is the approach I would take with AI.

1. I would use a chat tool Novelcrafter for most of the work, and possibly a chatbot like Claude to do my brainstorming

2. I would use the chatbot to do a little initial brain-

storming to give me some context, and to have an idea of the main character I'm writing.

3. I would then construct a style prompt for what I want the output to sound like. I would then use this style every time I start a new chapter.

4. As I discover new information about my characters or settings, I would input that information into Novelcrafter's codex to help improve the outline that the AI gives me

5. I would then write the chapters one beat at a time, with enough of a prompt to generate roughly 400-500 words of finished text.

6. I would edit that text, then feed it back into the AI to know what my changes were, and to get an idea of my more refined style.

7. And from there I would continue until I reached the end of the manuscript and edit as I normally would.

Summary:

- Discovery writers can still benefit from using AI tools like ChatGPT and Claude for brainstorming ideas, characters, settings, plot points, etc. to spark creativity before writing.

- Feed the AI one story beat at a time rather than a full outline. Edit the AI's output to your liking, then feed it back in to continue the story beat-by-beat.

- Experiment with the "Yes, but... No, and..." framework to find new and interesting ways to continue the story whilst still retaining the conflict.

- Tools like Sudowrite and Novelcrafter are both geared to work with discovery writing workflows

Part IV

AI Objections and Answers

Myth HQ, LLC

21

Why 99% of People Won't Even Read This

Welcome to my comprehensive list of every objection to AI and my answer to each of them, put as best as I can. I'm doing this not so those of us can have a way to argue with the cynics, but to have some peace of mind around our own choices to use AI, because I truly believe that AI is a wonderful tool and a godsend to anyone who has been struggling to write, such as those like myself with burnout, those with mental challenges, and more.

But I also know that most people who are AI-phobic not only won't listen or be convinced by any of these arguments, but they probably won't even read them (which is why I'm not encouraging you to copy/paste any of these arguments into your Facebook friend's feed).

I don't necessarily blame them, and this is why.

Because AI is scary, it has a lot of implications and it WILL disrupt the industry for good *and* for bad. And most people are afraid of this and will look for any excuse to fight against it.

For instance, my AI-phobic authors point out that AI is "stealing" copyrighted material. And part of this issue is that most of the AI developers did indeed use copyrighted work to train their models. But as we've seen with every court case brought against these companies so far, that's legal. The courts have been dismissing these cases left and right, so the AI developers did nothing illegal. And indeed, when you understand WHY these cases were thrown out, you'll understand why using copyrighted work in the training data is not stealing (see the next chapter).

Nevertheless, to authors who don't understand copyright law very well, it *feels* like theft. Someone took their work without their permission and used it to create something that's making them money.

It's completely understandable that it feels like theft.

But it's not.

Which is the crux of this issue. Most authors are using their emotions to drive their decisions instead of logic. And facts will never change the mind of someone whose position was based on emotion.

Even when you show AI developers that have clearly legally licensed their content and paid for all source material, even those people are under fire. For instance, Adobe has done everything by the book, and no one can argue that they're stealing anything for their AI models, and yet they get a ton of criticism for incorporating AI into their software anyway.

Why?

Because the issue isn't actually about copyright or so-called plagiarism. People are just scared.

And again, that's understandable. It takes a lot of work to become an artist, in any category. When a technology comes along that _feels_ (there's that word again) like it will replace the work that you do, suddenly it feels like we may all be out of a job soon, and that's terrifying.

And that's why most people who object to AI will not actually use these explanations I've compiled here. Because they've already made up their mind, and no amount of logic will convince them.

Most people fall under one of two mindsets: a scarcity mindset or an abundance mindset. Here's a brief explanation of both:

- **Scarcity Mindset:** Focuses on limitations and fear of not having enough, usually leading to anxiety and unhealthy competition. These people are often the same as those with a victim mindset, who believe that external factors have control over their lives and they are helpless against them.

- **Abundance Mindset**: Emphasizes possibilities and opportunities, usually leading to increased optimism and collaboration with others. These people are often synonymous with those of a creator mindset, which means they take personal responsibility and see challenges as opportunities.

Most of the AI-phobic artists and authors out there fall into the scarcity/victim mindset camp because they perceive AI as presenting an existential threat.

But for the abundance/creator-minded author, AI is more of an infinite opportunity, allowing us to do things that never would have been possible before.

So if you are reading this and you genuinely fear AI, I would invite you to try and temporarily set that aside and search for the potential opportunities in AI, something that might enable you to achieve more than what would have been possible without AI.

At the very least, I invite you to listen to some of these answers to the common objections about AI. I truly built this resource with a desire to properly address these concerns, and not to minimize them. I want to help us all understand this technology together, because we'll understand it better the more we learn about it.

And with that, let's get into some of the most common objections I've seen to AI technologies, and my answers to them, using the most reasonable and logical arguments that I know.

22

"AI is Stealing Other People's Work"

This is by far the most difficult question to answer, as there is both a legal and ethical perspective, and even if you can prove that using copyrighted work to train an AI is legal, many will still vehemently disagree that it's also ethical.

But I think that the ethical argument also has a certain amount to do with a misunderstanding of how AI works, although once again, this will probably not convince the anti-AI author who is set in their position.

However, I will do the best I can here to show how AI is acting in fair use, and therefore not stealing and totally legal (this is why all of the lawsuits brought against AI are getting thrown out), and also hopefully explain how AI works in such a way that it will be clear why I think it's completely ethical as well.

You are more than welcome to completely disagree with me. I even get quite a few pro-AI authors who agree that it's not the most ethical thing in the world to train a book on copyrighted material. I will even agree that it's a very gray area. But with that said, here's a bit more context on the subject...

Side note: *big thank you to Laura Crenshaw for pointing me to some examples and arguments around this specific concern.*

Understanding Fair Use

In the age of AI, we must understand the concept of fair use, especially with AI and copyright law. Fair use is a legal doctrine that allows for limited use of copyrighted material without permission from the copyright holder. It's a fundamental part of copyright law that balances the rights of creators with the public interest in the free flow of information and ideas.

Many people will argue that using AI for training purposes falls outside of Fair Use. But stick with me for a second.

What Is Fair Use?

Fair use is a legal safety valve that allows for the use of copyrighted material under certain circumstances. It's what allows us to quote other authors in our books, or for teachers to photocopy pages from textbooks for their students. Without fair use, creativity and innovation would be stifled, and we'd all be too scared to build upon the work of others.

But fair use isn't just about quoting a few lines or using a small portion of someone's work. It can actually cover much broader uses, including, potentially, the use of copyrighted works to train AI models. And based on certain legal precedents, there are several reasons why training AI on copyrighted work constitutes fair use:

You see, there are four key factors that judges and lawyers use when determining whether something falls under fair use:

1. Purpose and Character of Use

2. Nature of the Copyrighted Work

3. Amount and Substantiality of the Portion Used

4. Effect on the Potential Market or Value of the Work

Let's break these down one by one...

1. Purpose and Character of Use

This factor looks at whether the use of the copyrighted material is used for commercial or professional gain. Now this may sound, on the surface, like this would rule in favor of infringement, because these AI companies are obviously using these copyrighted materials to train a model that will make them money.

But it's unfortunately not that simple. Because for it to be clearly infringement, you have to prove that the use of the material is blatantly derivative, and not transformative. In other words, does it add something new, with a further purpose or different character, altering the first with new expression, meaning, or message?

Now, here's where it gets interesting for AI. When an AI model is trained on copyrighted works, it's not simply regurgitating those works. It's learning *mathematical* patterns, styles, and structures to create something entirely new. It's transforming the input into a complex mathematical model that can generate original text.

Think about it this way: when we read books to learn how to write, we're not copying those books word for word. We're learning patterns, styles, and structures to create our own original works. AI is doing the same thing, just on a much larger scale and much faster. And so it would seem that most of the uses of copyrighted works in an AI training dataset are transformative, meaning it won't be looked at as infringement...most likely.

2. Nature of the Copyrighted Work

This factor considers whether the copyrighted work is factual or creative. Generally, using factual works is more likely to be fair use than using highly creative works.

For AI training, this factor is a bit of a mixed bag. The datasets used to train AI models often include both factual and creative works. However, the purpose of using these works isn't to reproduce their creative elements, but to learn language patterns and structures. This could potentially tilt this factor in favor of fair use.

3. Amount and Substantiality of the Portion Used

This factor looks at how much of the copyrighted work is used, both quantitatively and qualitatively. Using a small portion of a work is more likely to be considered fair use than using the entire work.

Now, I know what you're thinking. "But Jason, AI models are trained on entire books! How can that possibly be fair use?" Here's the thing: while AI models are indeed trained on entire works, they cannot, by their nature, reproduce those works in their entirety. Instead, they learn from the patterns in the data to create a statistical model of language. At best, and only when forced by the user, an AI model can only produce small quotes from a book.

It's like how we as authors might read hundreds of books in our genre to understand the conventions and styles, but we're not copying those books when we write our own. We're using the knowledge we've gained to create something new. AI is doing the same thing, just on a much larger scale.

4. Effect on the Potential Market or Value of the Work

This final factor considers whether the use of the copyrighted material negatively impacts the market for the original work. If the use doesn't compete with or undermine the market for the original, it's more likely to be considered fair use.

Here's where I think AI has a strong case for fair use. When an AI model is trained on a book, it doesn't reproduce that book or create a substitute for it. The output of the AI is a new, original work. It doesn't compete with the books it was trained on any more than a human author's work competes with all the books they've read.

Historical Precedents for Fair Use

Now, let's look at some historical precedents that might shed light on how fair use applies to AI. One of the most interesting cases is Burrow-Giles Lithographic Co. v. Sarony from 1884.

This case was about whether photographs could be copyrighted. The court decided that yes, they could, because the photographer made "conscious choices" in creating the photo. The judge said that "mechanical capture was protected because conscious choices created something new."

Now, why is this relevant to AI? Well, when we use AI tools like ChatGPT or Midjourney, we're making conscious choices in our prompts, and in how we refine and edit the output. We're not just pushing a button and getting a fully-formed novel (like many in the anti-camp assume). We're actively engaged in a creative process, guiding the AI to help us create something new.

Another fascinating case is Google v. Oracle from 2021. In this case, Google had copied over 11,000 lines of code from Oracle's Java API for use in the Android operating system. The Supreme Court ruled that this was fair use, emphasizing that Google's use was transformative and contributed significantly to the progress of computer science.

This case is particularly relevant to AI because it shows that even using a substantial amount of copyrighted material can be considered fair use if it's transformative and contributes to progress in the field.

How AI Actually Works

Alright, let's dive into the nitty-gritty of how AI actually works. Understanding the basics of how these AI models function can really change your perspective on whether they're "stealing" work or not.

Let's break this down into two main categories: art generation and language models, since these are the most common forms of AI in creative fields. They work in a way that's actually quite similar to each other.

Art Generation

First, let's talk about AI art generation, like what you see with tools like Midjourney or DALL-E. Now, I'm not an artist myself, but as authors, many of us work with cover designers or illustrators, and I will often use AI for tasks like character concept art.

Many people think that AI art generators are just making a fancy collage out of all the images it's been trained on. First of all, if this were true, that would be legal, as collages are protected under fair use. I can, right now, go cut up pieces of 100% copyrighted materials and make a college, then go sell that collage for money.

But, when you give a prompt to an AI art tool, it's not just going through its database and copy-pasting bits of images together. Instead, it's trying to understand the concepts in your prompt and then generate an image that matches those concepts.

Here's how it works in simple terms:

1. The AI is trained on millions of images, each paired with text descriptions.

2. It learns to associate certain mathematical elements of certain visuals with specific words or phrases.

3. When you give it a prompt, it tries to create an image that matches the concepts in your prompt, based on what it's learned.

The AI isn't just cutting and pasting bits of the original images it was trained on. Instead, it's creating a sort of mathematical understanding of each concept. It's like the AI has built a geographical model of what a cat looks like, based on all the examples it's seen.

And it does this by creating a single pixel, then based on the mathematics of images that it's learned, it generates the pixel next to it, and that pixel is colored based on probability of what that pixel should look like, based on the text prompt the model was given. Then it continues to the next pixel, determines the probability of what it should look like, etc.

When you ask it to create an image, it's using these mental models to generate something new. It's not copying any single image from its training data, but rather using the mathematics of visual concepts to create something original.

However, and this is important to understand, AI art generators can sometimes produce outputs that look like existing copyrighted/trademarked images. For example, I can ask for an image of Pikachu dressed up like Batman, and it will probably create something that looks exactly like that prompt.

This is why, as authors, if we're using AI-generated art for our book covers or promotional materials, we need to be careful. It's our responsibility to make sure the output does not depict existing copyrighted works. Because if I tried to sell that image of Pikachu dressed as Batman, I could easily be sued by the owners of the copyright for those two intellectual properties, just like what would happen if I drew the image myself, or used Photoshop, and tried to sell it.

As with any tool, WE are responsible for what we produce with it, not the tool itself.

Word Vectors in Language Models

Now, let's move on to language models, which is probably what most of us authors are more interested in. These are the models behind tools like ChatGPT or Claude, which we might use for brainstorming, drafting, or editing.

Language models work quite similarly to art generation models. But instead of starting with one pixel then moving on to the next, they're building a complex (and once again, mathematical) understanding of how words relate to one another.

A large language models don't actually understand words as we do. They work with something called "word vectors."

Imagine each word as a point in a vast, multi-dimensional space. Words with similar meanings are closer together in this space. For example, "peanut" and "butter" might be close together, and both might be relatively close to "allergy," but far from "democracy."

When a language model is trained, it's essentially learning the positions of all these words in this multi-dimensional space. But it's not just learning individual words - it's learning the relationships between words, phrases, and even larger chunks of text.

Here's a simplified version of how it works:

1. The model is trained on a massive amount of text data.

2. It learns to predict what word is likely to come next in a sequence.

3. Through this process, it builds up its understanding of word relationships and language patterns.

Now, here's the crucial part: when you ask a language model to generate text, it's not just copying and pasting from its training data. It's using its understanding of language patterns to generate new text that fits those patterns.

For example, if I ask you to complete this sentence: "I want ice cream with chocolate and peanut BLANK" you automatically know that the likely word to come next is "butter".

Additionally, if I tell you to complete this sentence: "I went to the hospital because of my peanut BLANK", you can guess that the next word will be "allergy".

Both words come after the word "peanut", but since we've learned language effectively, we're able to determine from the context of the sentence, the word that has the highest *probability* of coming next. Now it's entirely possible that I meant to say "peanut ceiling fan" but that would be, from a probability standpoint, very unlikely.

AI is looking at words in the same way. It judges what the *probability* of the next word is, based on the prompt it was given, and the words that came before. It's literally just mathematically building a piece of text one word at a time.

And all that is happening when a LLM is being trained on a book, even a copyrighted book, is that the word vectors in this multi-dimensional space are shifting slightly as it learns new word associations.

It's a bit like how we, as human authors, write. We don't copy-paste sentences from books we've read. Instead, we've internalized the patterns of language and storytelling from everything we've read, and we use that knowledge to create something new.

This is why, when you use a tool like ChatGPT, you'll often get different results each time, even if you ask the same question. The model isn't retrieving a stored answer; it's generating a new response each time based on its understanding of language patterns.

And in fact, for both art and language AI training, there is no storage of copyrighted work after the fact. That's why someone can literally take some of the smaller models and run them completely from their computer. Yes, the amount of data used to train a model may number in the terabytes, but the resulting model itself doesn't have any of that data, and only takes up a few gigabytes of space, hence why the smaller models can run locally on anyone's computer.

If a model were somehow maintaining a huge database of copyrighted information and images, no one would be able to run these models, as it would take up far too much space and compute power to retrieve all that information when prompted.

Transformative Nature of AI Outputs

Now that we understand a bit about how these AI models work, let's talk about why their outputs are transformative. This is crucial to the fair use argument we discussed earlier.

In both art and text generation, AI is not simply reproducing its training data. It's using that data to build a complex understanding of visual concepts or language patterns and then using that understanding to create something new.

Let's break this down:

1. **Originality:** Each output from an AI model is unique. Even if you give the same prompt multiple times, you'll get different results. This is because the AI isn't retrieving stored information, but generating new content each time.

2. **Synthesis of Multiple Sources:** AI models are trained on vast amounts of data from numerous sources. Any single output is a synthesis of information from many different sources, combined in a way that's unique to that particular prompt and generation.

3. **Adaptation to New Contexts:** AI can apply its learned knowledge to new situations that weren't explicitly part of its training data. For example, you could ask GPT to write a story in the style of Shakespeare but set in our future. Shakespeare never wrote about the future, but the AI can combine its understanding of Shakespeare's style with its knowledge of futuristic concepts to create something entirely new.

4. **Interaction with User Input:** The output of AI models is heavily influenced by the prompts and interactions from the user. As authors, when we use AI tools, we're not just passively receiving output from the AI. We're actively guiding it, refining its outputs, and combining its suggestions with our own ideas. The final product is a collaboration between human and AI creativity.

5. **Inability to Reproduce Training Data:** This is a big one. AI models, particularly large language models, are generally incapable of reproducing large chunks of their training data verbatim. They're designed to generate new text based on patterns, not to retrieve and reproduce existing text.

Now, I know some of you might be thinking, "But Jason, I've heard of cases where AI has produced text that's identical to something in its training data!" And you're right, this can happen, but it's extremely rare, especially for longer pieces of text.

When it does happen, it's usually for very common phrases or for highly specific prompts that might only have a few examples in the training data.

For longer pieces of text, the chances of an AI reproducing something verbatim from its training data are **astronomically low.** It's far more likely that a human would accidentally plagiarize something they've read than for an AI to reproduce a significant chunk of text from its training data.

Now, I want to address a concern that I know many authors have. Some worry that AI will be able to mimic their specific style so well that it could essentially "steal" their voice. I get it. As authors, our voice is one of our most valuable assets.

But here's the thing: even if an AI could perfectly mimic your style (which current models can't do consistently), it still wouldn't be you. It wouldn't have your experiences, your emotions, your unique perspective on the world. Those are the things that truly make your writing yours.

Moreover, style is not copyrightable. If it were, we'd have to throw out huge swaths of genre fiction where authors deliberately write in similar styles. The value in your work isn't just in your style, but in the unique stories you tell and the perspectives you bring.

But Is it Ethical?

Now we come to the big question: Is using copyrighted material to train an AI model ethical?

We've certainly established that it falls under fair use, since no one (so far) has been able to prove that the resulting output from an AI is anything but transformative. And since it is transformative, it is 100% legal to do.

But there's certainly something that "feels" like stealing, no?

Here's my take: <u>using copyrighted material to train AI is unethical IF it can be proven to cause harm.</u>

That's where I draw the line on what is ethical or not.

And yet, if we can more or less prove (as these court cases are actively doing) that an AI uses copyrighted materials in transformative ways, doesn't that also prove that there is no harm being done by these models?

Of course, you might shoot back at that idea by saying that people *are* losing their jobs because people are replacing them with AI instead. While there are/will continue to be instances like this, I don't think we can say that the job loss was a result of using copyrighted material in the data set. AI technology will continue to exist, even if the courts decide that they can't use copyrighted material in the training data, because there is plenty of free data out there, or easily licensable data, or data that would be willingly donated by those who don't care.

Aka, the technology will continue to exist, and *that's* the reason why people are losing their jobs, not because the model is using someone's style. Excluding copyrighted material in the dataset will, at best, slow down the progress of the AI training, but is a far cry from stopping it.

And while this is certainly not universally true, and there will always be exceptions, what we're seeing is that instead of artists losing their jobs to AI, their jobs are merely transforming to include a lot more AI, which in turn decreases the time it takes to do a job, which decreases the price of the job, which then leads to growth in the market.

For example, many people who worked as translators are using AI to help them in the first draft of a translation, which saves them a ton of time to create a full translation. That time saving means they can also charge less, which actually INCREASES the market for translations. Before, many people wouldn't get translations because it was too expensive, but now they can, even professional ones.

So while there will certainly be shifts in the market, and in the case of AI, radical shifts, AI is much more likely to actually increase markets over time, as more and more people realize what's possible now that the time costs have come down.

So is it unethical? I think we can make an argument that the transformative nature of AI makes it not harmful, and indeed, it's nearly impossible to get AI to plagiarize someone else's work without a human forcibly prompting it to do so.

It chooses a response, token by token, or pixel by pixel, in a math equation based on probability.

Now, if someone somehow intentionally plagiarizes with AI and then made money from that, then that would be unethical. But that's holding the end user responsible, not the company. Just like how Amazon wouldn't be responsible for plagiarism if I took a book that I bought on Amazon and used it in an academic paper without citing it.

As users of these technologies, it is 100% our responsibility to make sure we are using them ethically.

Ultimately, this is a really hot philosophical issue, and just because I tend to lean on the side of it being completely legal AND ethical, does not mean that everyone will.

However, based on what I know of how AI works and how fair use works, I truly can't see the harm that is caused by AI that would spark claims of it not being ethical. In my mind, there has to be proof of harm by specifically using copyrighted work in the dataset, which no one has yet to adequately convince me of yet.

Why I Don't Think the "Stealing" Argument Will Be Relevant for Long

Funny enough, even after that very long response, I actually don't think the "stealing" argument is all that relevant, or at least, it won't continue to be for much longer. Here are a few reasons why:

1. Synthetic Training Data

Companies like Nvidia are creating AI models that specifically generate training data. This means that in the future, 90% of what a company uses to train their AI might not even be human-created material. They're managing to do this without succumbing to the problems of AI self-referential learning or "AI Model Collapse".

This shift towards synthetic data could significantly reduce the reliance on copyrighted material for training.

2. Compensation for Data Licensing is Already Starting Without Government Interference

We're seeing a trend of tech companies making deals with content providers. Reddit, News Corp, and many others have already established deals with big tech companies like OpenAI and Google, even if it's not legally required.

This is likely a strategy to avoid controversy and potential legal battles. It's probably just a matter of time before we see some form of compensation system for authors and artists whose work is used in AI training, although I imagine the big content providers like traditional publishers, news outlets, and Hollywood companies will likely get that compensation long before the individual artist does. But that's a fight for a future time.

3. Ethical Training Methods

Some companies are pursuing 100% legal and increasingly ethical avenues for AI training. For example, we're seeing more datasets come up like the Common Corpus training dataset, which is sourced entirely from public domain content and creative commons material, like CC YouTube videos and the like. There's actually quite a lot of training data there, so it's likely that AI would be able to continue its advancements between this ethically sourced material and the synthetic training data mentioned above.

Additionally, there's Adobe's approach of training on their own in-house data in the Adobe Stock library, which they clearly have the rights to use. These methods prove that it's possible to create powerful AI models without using copyrighted material without permission.

4. LLM Improvements

One argument that AI-phobic authors will put out is that training data is eventually going to run out for these companies, meaning they will only be able to train these models to a certain limit, after which the models simply won't be able to improve, and the advancement of LLMs will be stunted.

This is simply not true, and a misunderstanding of how these models work.

What these authors miss is that AI developers have long been aware that training data can only take them so far, and for a long time. In fact, in March 2023 (around when GPT-4 was released) Sam Altman even announced that *large* language models were probably a dead-end, and they were going to need to find ways to improve the models without throwing terabytes of content at them.

And they've already proven they can do that.

A good example (as of this writing) is GPT-4o, which had very little additional training, but now it is much improved in its abilities, including improved reasoning and math skills.

And that's what's important here, the fact that the training data is only part of the equation. The other part is just improving the systems and the technology so that you're able to do more with less, i.e. make an even smarter LLM with the same, or even less, training data.

Plus, add to that the fact that synthetic training data is now a thing, a "limit" to the amount of training data is not going to be an issue in the future.

5. Smaller Models and Personal AI

In the near future, it will probably be possible for individuals to train their own AI models on whatever content they choose. It's already possible to fine-tune open source models with copyrighted material, meaning anyone could make an

LLM based around any author's writing style in their basement, as long as they have a powerful enough machine.

This decentralization of AI training will make it nearly impossible for governments to enforce laws requiring the exclusion of copyrighted material in training data.

Instead, the focus will likely shift to enforcing output - preventing plagiarism in the final product. But as we've established, it's very difficult to accidentally plagiarize with AI without intentional prompting. All output is largely considered transformative at worst, and completely original at best, meaning there would be no enforcement necessary.

23

"Using AI Removes Creativity"

This is another really common concern, with a lot of artists and authors wondering why anyone would use AI because it sort of defeats the point of creativity. At least, that's what they think.

Personally, I found that this concern more or less melts away the moment you start to actually work with these tools as the productivity tools that they are. But for those who need more convincing, here are a few thoughts.

The Photography Parallel

This isn't the first time we've heard this argument. Back when photography was the new kid on the block, people said much the same thing. "That's not art!" they cried, clutching their paintbrushes. It took a while for photography to be recognized as a legitimate art form, worthy of copyright protection.

Then we got the Burrow-Giles Lithographic Co. v. Sarony case of 1884. This legal showdown was about whether photographs could be copyrighted. The court said yes, because the photographer made "conscious choices" in creating the photo.

And now we know that photography is much more than just pressing a button (although it can be just that). It involves positioning the subject, choosing the perfect lighting condition, adjusting all the camera's settings, etc.

Yes, there are a lot of photos that are not very artistic. The 16th selfie that you took next to the Eiffel Tower probably won't win any awards. But just because some photography isn't art, doesn't mean all photograph isn't art. That would be silly.

Prompting

Fast forward to today, and we're having the same debate about AI. But here's the thing: using AI is all about conscious choices, possibly even more so than photography. It's not just "Computer, make art!" and poof, a masterpiece appears.

Prompting an AI is like developing film in a darkroom. It takes skill, patience, and a lot of trial and error. You're constantly tweaking, adjusting, and fine-tuning to get the result you want. And even then, you might not be satisfied and need to start over.

And after you've got your AI-generated base, there's still reviewing, editing, and modifying to be done. It's your vision driving the process, not the AI's (which doesn't even have one).

The Human Touch

At the end of the day, it's still your creativity, your ideas, your vision that's being brought to life. The AI is just another tool in your creative arsenal, like a really smart paintbrush or a camera that can read your mind (badly).

Sure, there will be folks who use AI with little to no human oversight. But let's be real - those people aren't our competition. They're far more likely to fall into obscurity and never get noticed, because those actually pairing the AI with their hard work and creative oversight are always going to come out on top.

I'll have more to say on this in the section on market saturation.

The Art Spectrum

Human creativity is still at the heart of working with AI. But just like with photography, there's a spectrum of what we'd consider "art". The blurry selfie I took of my bed head this morning isn't exactly Ansel Adams material. (Or is it? Maybe

I've accidentally created a masterpiece of modern art. Quick, someone call the Louvre!)

On the other end of the spectrum, you've got folks spending hours crafting the perfect prompt, tweaking every parameter, and then painstakingly editing the results to match their vision. That's creativity, folks, even if a machine helped along the way.

The Bottom Line

Using AI doesn't remove creativity any more than using a camera or a paintbrush does. It's just another tool, albeit a pretty fancy one. What matters is how you use it, the choices you make, and the vision you bring to the table.

So the next time someone tells you AI removes creativity, ask them if they think the same about cameras. Then show them your artsy bed head selfie. That'll convince them for sure.

24

"If You Write with AI, You're Not a Writer"

T his thought typically comes from a misunderstanding of how AI writing works and how humans practically interact with it.

If you watch any of the videos on my channel, you'll realize that writing with AI is different than just pushing a button and getting a book.

Even the most hands-off approach to using AI to do the bulk of the writing usually requires EXTENSIVE editing by the human afterward. Without it, the book is garbage, and you don't need to worry about garbage replacing you.

But what people who say this don't realize is that writing with AI is a **collaborative** process.

People have been collaborating in other ways for centuries. Collaboration like this includes (but is not limited to):

- Co-writing with another author

- Participating in a writer's room

- Using plotting software or plotting templates

- Hiring an editor or book coach

And that's just scratching the surface. Other forms of storytelling (i.e. film, television, video games, comics) require a lot more collaboration.

AI is the same.

AI is not replacing writers, it is not writing the bulk of the book for you. Anyone who has actually used AI knows this.

It is, instead, a productivity and collaborative tool, to bounce ideas off of, help you write the next few paragraphs if you get stuck, or even produce an entire first draft so you can go in there and edit it (and yes, it almost always requires substantial edits).

The end result is a patchwork where you're unable to tell where the AI ended and the human began. But ultimately, these tools do not work without the human guiding them. So it's still the human steering the ship, and therefore still the human that wrote the book.

25

"You Can't Copyright AI Work"

T his is one of the most-asked questions that I get, even from AI-positive authors. Let's try to make sense of it.

The Copyright Confusion

Let's clear up a common misconception, it's not true that you can't copyright any work that involves AI. First of all, there is a growing number of countries that are granting copyright to AI-generated works.

For example, the United Kingdom, Japan, New Zealand, and China all allow copyright. So you're welcome to file copyright in those countries and sue anyone who wants to try and sell your AI-generated work in those countries (which, admittedly, is unlikely to happen anyway).

In other countries, such as the U.S., you can still file copyright for a work that has used AI elements, but the arrangement and placement of those elements are your own. So for example, a comic book where you took AI images and arranged them in a certain way with text. Those specific images are public domain, but your use of the images can be copyrighted, ultimately resulting in a product that's more or less of the same legal status of another book.

For AI-text, it's even harder for the copyright office (and even for you) to determine what elements of a written piece were developed with AI, and which were written by you. It's usually a patchwork of both, and entirely impossible to know where the AI ends and the human begins.

How Should You File Copyright?

In the U.S. Copyright guidance for AI, it says this in Page 5, Paragraph A:

> Individuals who use AI technology in creating a work may claim copyright protection for their own contributions to that work. They must use the Standard Application, and in it identify the author(s) and provide a brief statement in the "Author Created" field that describes the authorship that was contributed by a human. For example, an applicant who incorporates AI-generated text into a larger textual work should claim the portions of the textual work that is human-authored. And an applicant who creatively arranges the human

and non-human content within a work should fill out the "Author Created" field to claim: "Selection, coordination, and arrangement of [describe human authored content] created by the author and [describe AI content] generated by artificial intelligence." Applicants should not list an AI technology or the company that provided it as an author or co-author simply because they used it when creating their work.

The good news is, while you do need to list that you used AI for *portions* of the book you wrote, or the art you created, you don't have to get too specific. You don't have to say 17% was AI and 83% was human. All you have to do is claim the selection, coordination, and arrangement of your human content as created by you, using elements generated by artificial intelligence.

Also, whatever you do, don't list the AI as the author, because an AI can't be the author. Only humans can receive copyright notice. And here's why...

Who Should Own Copyright?

We actually have some precedent for why AI has not been able to gain copyright in some areas. For instance, do you know who owns the copyright for every photo you take? It's whomever actually pushed the button. That means when you're on a trip and you ask someone to take a picture of you and your family, that random stranger is technically the copyright holder of that photo, even if it's not their camera.

But one thing that's pretty clear among many different copyright laws is that only humans are allowed to hold copyright. So what happens if a monkey were to push the button and take a selfie?

Well, that's exactly the question that came up in the Slater Monkey Case (2015) where a monkey accidentally took a selfie using a camera, and then when the owner of the camera tried to get copyright, the results differed depending on the country. For example:

- In the United States it's clear that animals cannot hold copyright, so since the human did not push the button, it was decided that no one owns the copyright.

- In the United Kingdom, they determined that in the absence of a human author, the next closest human should own the copyright, meaning the owner of the camera (as the human closest to the image) managed to secure the copyright in the UK.

This is one of the reasons why the UK allows for AI to be copyrighted, because they allow something not created by a human still be copyrighted by the human who is essentially next in line, or who makes the most sense to be the copyright holder.

And in the case of AI, the closest human would be the person who prompted the AI to get the results that the AI gave.

Why I Believe the U.S. Copyright Policy Will Almost Certainly Change

I'm still, honestly, a bit confused by why the copyright office in the U.S. still doesn't allow the prompter to own copyright over the AI output resulting from the prompt, but I think it comes down to one major misconception:

AI is not actually intelligent.

There's a misguided idea in our culture in general that Artificial Intelligence actually has some kind of mind of its own. Right now, it doesn't. It's nothing more than a tool, with no mind to speak of. It's completely innert without human guidance, hence, it is a tool.

And yet, the copyright office has no problem with you claiming copyright on work you created with other tools? For example, if you created a piece of photo manipulation art in Adobe Photoshop, you could absolutely copyright that content. So why not a tool like AI? It's still a tool, albeit an advanced one. But there's still no intelligence there, meaning that all output is the direct result of human intervention.

When you realize that all it takes to get the copyright of a photograph is to push the button (which is not very much creative input at all), it suddenly becomes confusing why a prompt to an AI would not receive the same level of copyright designation. After all, most prompts take a lot more creative input than simply pushing the button of a camera.

So I'm of the opinion that, as those in the copyright office become more aware of how AI actually works, and that there's no actual intelligence behind it, it won't be long before the United States changes their policies.

Plus, China is allowing copyright, and the United States is bound to feel pressure to compete with that. So we'll see.

26

"Authors/Artists Who Use AI Are Taking Jobs Away From Hard-working Authors/Artists"

This is another hot-spot topic for a lot of authors. Because technology *always* results in shifts in the market that lead to job loss, job transformation, and the creation of new jobs.

And AI is one of those areas where the amount of shift in the market is higher than normal, so a lot of people are really feeling the effect of it.

To really wrap our heads around this one, let me try to use an analogy.

But first, you've all heard the phrase "work smarter, not harder," which is good advice overall. But would you agree that it's even better to work "smarter AND harder"?

Well then, imagine we have four different authors:

- **Lazy Larry:** who wants to be a writer, but either isn't willing to put any of the work into it, or learn what is needed to succeed. He writes now and then when the muse strikes, but has no consistency and the amount of time he puts into his work is miniscule.

- **Get Rich Quick Gwen:** Gwen is a lot like Larry, she doesn't like to put in a lot of work, but still wants to find success anyway, so she's constantly taken in by talk of the "get rich quick" schemes, and promises of the magic pill that will automatically launch her to stardom. But like Larry, she doesn't put in the time it takes to actually get good at her craft, and continues to see very little success. Despite that, Gwen takes pride in being the person who works "smarter, not harder."

- **Hard Work Harold:** Then we get Hard Work Harold, and this guy is a hard worker. He spends hours and hours writing and, as a result, has amassed dozens of books in his back catalogue. He spends hours and hours learning his craft and slaving away, and he has no time for any of the "get rich quick" talk because he knows that true success comes from hard work and dedication. He can't be bothered with anything else, and he looks down at anyone who claims they've found the magic pill.

- **Tech-savvy Tiffany:** Tiffany differs from all three of

the others. Not only is she a hard worker, but she's also good at staying up to date with the latest technology. She is constantly looking for new opportunities, much like Gwen does, but couples that with a strong work ethic. As a result of her hard work, she is not only just as prolific as Harold, and just as good in her craft, but she's also more likely to see opportunity and be able to capitalize on it than Harold is, because all he's concerned with is just working harder. Tiffany is the epitome of working "smarter, AND harder."

Now let's say we could somehow quantify the level of success that these people have on a numbered scale, with 0 being the lowest, and 10+ being the highest. Now, of course, it's never that simple with real people, but bear with me for a moment.

Given the profiles above, let's say Lazy Larry had a success rate of 2 because he's not very smart and he's also not a hard worker. Get Rich Quick Gwen does a little better, at maybe a 4, because even though she has about the same work ethic as Larry, her obsession with getting rich quick actually leads to a number of ways to work that are "smarter, not harder."

Side note: don't be too quick to dismiss the "get rich quick" schemes. Always use good judgement, because some are just scams, but many are actually legitimate ways to work smarter, not harder. And even though they might not get you rich quick as promised, they can usually find a way to make your work a bit easier.

Now let's look at Hard Work Harold. Because he works hard and has a lot of experience, he benefits from that greatly, with a success metric around an 8. Tech-savvy Tiffany starts out around the same, about an 8. However, when the right technology comes around, she sees an opportunity and takes advantage of that, leading her to a higher success rate of 10 or even higher.

Now, of course, I'm simplifying here. But we have seen over and over again that those who embrace technology tend to have more success overall. We saw this recently with the rise of self-publishing. Those that saw the opportunity and got in on the ground floor were the first to succeed big. And those that were willing to work hard *in addition* to the benefits of the technology hit it even bigger.

So let's apply this to AI. With these four examples, here's a picture of what might happen.

- **Lazy Larry:** Larry gets completely left behind, as he was not a very hard worker anyway, and AI just made that gap wider. I imagine many of the people losing their jobs fall into this camp. The work they produced was not great to begin with, and with someone coming along who could do better with AI, the writing was on the wall.

- **Get Rich Quick Gwen:** Gwen does a little better. She sees AI as an opportunity and starts to produce tons and tons of books. But none of these books are very good, because she isn't willing to put in the work to make them good, or to learn her craft. So while she does marginally better than Larry, she is ultimately left behind as well, as the market adjusts and only the best manages to keep the good jobs.

- **Hard Work Harold:** Harold actually has a chance of remaining at the top. Embracing technology is not always required for success, and Harold's strong work ethic goes a long way in keeping him afloat. All the "crap" produced by the Gwens of the world does nothing to Harold, because none of them are able to reach the same level of quality as his. However, he's still unable to produce more or improve the quality of his work more than he could do before. His ability to 10x his business is severely limited because he's too focused on the hard work to realize that he may be putting too much effort into tasks that he could make easier if he embraced AI.

- **Tech-savvy Tiffany:** Tiffany, on the other hand, succeeds the best. She embraces AI *and* puts a lot of hard work into her craft. Because of this, even others like Gwen can't come close to her. Because while Gwen is embracing AI as well, that advantage is completely negated by the fact that Tiffany combines the advantages of AI with hard work. Tiffany also eventually outshines Harold, because they both have the same work ethic, but Tiffany was willing to find ways to make her author business easier to grow and manage through the use of AI and other technologies.

So in these scenarios, it's the people who embrace the technology AND have strong work ethics that succeed the most.

Now you might say, "that's fine Jason, but just because it works for your made up examples, that doesn't mean it works in a real-world scenario."

Except it does.

The most successful storytellers of all time were the people who embraced technology:

- Walt Disney built a storytelling empire around new technologies like animation, television, and many, many more.

- George Lucas wowed the world in Star Wars with the innovations that he pioneered in visual effects through ILM, the company he founded.

- J. K. Rowling could have made far less from the Harry Potter books had she not refused to let digital ebook rights fall into a publisher's hands. Instead, she saw the opportunity just as ebooks were becoming a thing, and decided to self-publish the ebook versions of the Harry Potter books herself, making her the richest author in the world.

- Many authors found their first success when self-publishing was first introduced by Amazon. Over time, it became harder and harder to break in with self-publishing, but by that time the early adopters had grown their audiences large enough to sustain their author careers (if they were smart).

And that's just a small sample. Almost every successful entrepreneur and storyteller saw some kind of opportunity and took advantage of it. This is actually something I teach to my students called the Red Car principle, the act of looking for opportunity when most people are just letting it pass them by. But those who are looking for the opportunity are the "lucky" ones, those who find success because they were actually looking for it.

AI is the same, and we will eventually see that those that don't embrace the technology will eventually fall behind. Because it will only take a few more years before AI is commonplace everywhere (it already is, to a degree). So be the Tech-savvy Tiffany, not the other three.

27

"This Time, It's Different..."

Now, despite everything I've said in the previous answer, many authors claim that "this time, it's different."

You see, it's common for those of us who are Pro-AI to point to new inventions in writing technology like the printing press, typewriters, the personal computer, the Internet, etc. as just other examples of different tools that made the writing process easier, more convenient, and more available to the underprivileged (because yes, being able to write is a privilege). And we like to point to AI and say that this is just another tool in a long line of tools that have made our jobs easier.

And if you actually work with AI, you'll know this to be true. It's much more of a productivity tool *for* writers, rather than a replacement *of* writers. And that is exactly how it should be used, as a productivity tool, to get your vision out of your head and onto "paper" faster than before.

And yet, so many authors think that this time it's different.

No, it's not.

And it becomes more and more apparent that it's not when we actually look back at the reactions to each of these different technologies when they were first invented. Here are some examples of technologies that have affected writing and art.

- **The Printing Press:** Scribes feared job loss and religious leaders worried about the spread of heretical ideas. The Ottoman Empire even banned printing presses for over 200 years to maintain control over information.

- **The Typewriter:** Some writers claimed it would ruin the art of writing. Mark Twain bought one and said, "After a year or two I found that it was degrading my character...full of caprices, full of defects — devilish ones."

- **Photography:** Painters feared obsolescence, claiming photos lacked artistic merit. Charles Baudelaire called it "art's most mortal enemy" in 1859.

- **The Digital Camera:** Film enthusiasts insisted digital could never match film quality. Kodak, once a giant in the industry, initially resisted the shift, even though it owned a patent on a digital camera that could have made them millions, but their delay eventually led to bankruptcy.

- **Adobe Photoshop:** Artists worried it would cheapen their craft. Some news outlets banned its use in photojournalism, fearing manipulation of truth. I've personally heard a lot of stories from artists who began making art in the early days of Photoshop, and how they were often shunned as "hacks" because they used Photoshop.

- **The Personal Computer:** Critics argued it would lead to job losses and social isolation. "Computerphobia" was in full swing.

- **The Internet:** Privacy advocates warned of data breaches, while some predicted the death of traditional media. The "Millennium Bug" panic of 1999 showcased widespread tech anxiety, all for nothing. Though oddly enough, this may be the technology responsible for the most damage of the bunch, based on more recent studies of the effects of social media, cyber bullying, pornography, and much more on younger generations, and yet no one would dare suggest we remove it from our society at this point.

- **The Self-publishing Movement:** Traditional publishers and some authors claimed it would flood the market with low-quality books. There's a brilliant response to this sentiment by author J. A. Konrath, titled "The Tsunami of Crap" where he showed the fallacy of thinking of the flood of low-quality self-published books as a threat.

Every single one of these technologies was an existential threat to *somebody*. However, for those that were able to adapt and follow the changes, those were able to ride the wave and still find that success.

AI is not different, other than perhaps having a more accelerated rate of improvement, merely requiring more adaptation.

But the sentiment that most AI-phobic authors tend to espouse is much the same as the "Tsunami of Crap" mentality that accompanied the early days of self-publishing. This was coming from established authors who ALSO thought that their careers were in danger (to be fair, they were if they weren't willing to adapt) and felt threatened by Amazon opening the doors to the public so anyone could self-publishing, thereby ending their privileged place in the publishing industry.

Again, each of these technologies was threatening because they increased accessibility to a less privileged population, from the printing press where the privilege was obvious, to self-publishing, which allowed anyone to publish without the need of the gatekeepers in traditional publishing.

AI is also allowing more people to open doors they couldn't open before, thus taking the privilege away from those who could. I see this every day from commenters who thank me for my instructions, because they're finally able to write their books that they've been wanting to write for years, but couldn't due to neurodivergence, physical handicaps, brain fog, burnout, ADHD and much more.

Yes, it's going to increase the number of people writing books and creating art. But so has every huge leap forward in technology before now.

And this time, nothing is different.

28

"AI Will Oversaturate the Market"

This is one of the big fears, that having so many AI-written books on the market will saturate the market, thereby making it impossible for legitimate books to stand out in a world where there's so much crap out there.

There are three primary reasons why this actually isn't a big deal AT ALL.

1. The market was already saturated

2. The solution to saturation is simple: don't produce crap

3. Money and marketing are the great equalizers

Let's dive into each of these.

1. The Market Was Already Saturated

Let's face it, the book market has been drowning in a sea of titles for years now. Amazon's algorithm is already dealing with millions of new books each year. And guess what? Most of them never see a single sale.

Why? Because Amazon's pretty darn good at filtering out the crap. They've had years to perfect their system. It's like a bouncer at an exclusive club, but instead of checking IDs, it's checking for quality content.

Remember when everyone freaked out about self-publishing? "Oh no, now anyone can publish a book!" they cried. Well, we survived that tsunami of mediocrity, didn't we? The cream still rose to the top.

The truth is, AI isn't going to suddenly flood the market with masterpieces. Most AI-generated books will be just as ignored as the majority of self-published works. The algorithm doesn't care if a human or a robot wrote the book – it cares if people are buying and enjoying it.

2. The Solution to Saturation is Simple: Don't Produce Crap

In the last concern, I mentioned J. A. Konrath's blog post on the "Tsunami of Crap." Well in that blog post, he proposed a solution that is just as relevant today for the AI concerns, as it was for the self-publishing concerns of the time:

> If you're really worried about readers being subjected to crap, here's what you can do:

DON'T WRITE CRAP.

But enough with the whining about it. It makes you look silly.

The authors who will succeed in an AI-saturated market are the same ones who succeed now: those who create quality content. If you're putting your heart and soul into your work, editing it carefully, and producing something you're proud of, you're already leagues ahead of any mass-produced AI drivel. It doesn't matter if you used AI in the process, as long as the end result is high quality.

Remember, readers aren't stupid. They can tell the difference between a book that's been crafted with care and one that's been hastily cobbled together by an algorithm. Give your readers some credit.

And if, for whatever reason, AI *does* start to produce books that readers like with little to no human oversight, I'm still not worried, because if it can do that on its own, just think of what it could do *with* a human. Human + AI will always be more powerful than either one alone.

3. Money and Marketing Are the Great Equalizers

Here's the kicker: most people who are producing massive amounts of crappy books in bulk—whether through AI or not—aren't able to put their money or time where their mouth is when it comes to marketing.

Marketing a book successfully requires more than just throwing it on Amazon and hoping for the best. It takes time, effort, and often, a decent chunk of change. And here's the thing: for marketing to be successful in the long run, you need to have a decent product.

You can't build a sustainable author brand on a foundation of low-quality, mass-produced books. Readers might fall for it once, but they won't come back for more. And in the book world, **repeat customers are the key to long-term success.**

Those churning out hundreds of AI-generated books a month? They can't afford the time or money it takes to really create a proper brand for each one. They're playing a numbers game, hoping that quantity will make up for quality.

But the authors who are willing to invest in their work—both in terms of creating a quality product and marketing it effectively—will immediately jump to the top 1% of all authors.

So, what's the bottom line here?

AI might change how some people approach writing, but it's not going to fundamentally alter the publishing landscape. Quality will always matter. Marketing will always matter. And most importantly, connecting with your readers will always matter.

Do those things, and you won't need to compete with a single author, because your readers will want YOU, and no one else can be you.

29

"ART SHOULD BE HARD"

Remember our old friend Hard-work Harold from the "Authors and Artists are Losing Jobs" objection? Well, he's back, and this time he's got a bone to pick with the idea that art might be getting easier. "Art should be hard!" he proclaims.

But should it, really?

Now, don't get me wrong. I'm all for putting in the effort. Hard work is admirable, and it often leads to the best results. But there's a difference between working hard and insisting that the process itself must be difficult. Let's dive into why the "art should be hard" mentality might be doing more harm than good.

The Self-Fulfilling Prophecy of Difficulty

Here's a fun fact: telling yourself something will be hard is a great way to make sure it actually is hard.

This phenomenon is related to self-efficacy, a fancy term psychologists use to describe your belief in your ability to succeed in specific situations. When you believe a task will be difficult, you're essentially lowering your self-efficacy. And guess what happens when you do that? You're less likely to even try, and if you do try, you're more likely to give up when you face the first hurdle.

It's a self-fulfilling prophecy. You believe art is hard, so you approach it with trepidation. You struggle more than necessary, reinforcing your belief that art is indeed hard. It's a vicious cycle, and before you know it, you're stuck in the "art is hard" quicksand.

The Blinders of Difficulty

But let's say you push through that initial resistance. You've accepted that art is hard, and you're ready to tackle it head-on. Good for you, right? Well, not so fast.

When you're convinced that something must be difficult, you're less likely to look for ways to make it easier. It's like wearing blinders that only let you see the hard path ahead. You might miss out on tools, techniques, or technologies that could streamline your process and make your art more enjoyable and efficient.

I see this happening all the time, and it's one of the things I warn authors about in my membership. Instead, you want to cultivate the "Red Car Principle". For instance, you've probably seen a red car sometime today, but you also probably don't remember it. But what if I told you that when you see a red car, I will pay you $50 for each one you spot? Then suddenly you're seeing red cars everywhere. This is what "luck" is. People aren't just lucky. They are looking for opportunity, even if they don't quite know it.

And when you're telling yourself that art should be hard, you are blinding yourself to all those potential opportunities.

Embracing the "Lazy" Route

What if I told you that being "lazy" could actually make you more effective? It was none other than Bill Gates, who famously said: "I choose a lazy person to do a hard job. Because a lazy person will find an easy way to do it."

Gates wasn't advocating for slacking off. He was recognizing the value of efficiency. "Lazy" people (in this context) are often the ones who find innovative solutions because they're motivated to reduce unnecessary effort. They're the ones who automate repetitive tasks, streamline workflows, and find shortcuts that save time and energy.

In the context of art, being "lazy" might mean embracing new technologies or techniques that make the creative process more efficient. It might mean using AI to help with brainstorming or to handle tedious tasks, freeing up more time for the truly creative aspects of your work.

The key is to channel that "laziness" into finding smarter ways to work, not avoiding work altogether. It's about maximizing your creative output while minimizing unnecessary struggle.

Working Smarter, Not Just Harder

Here's where we bring it all together. The goal shouldn't be to make art hard for the sake of being hard. The goal should be to create the best art possible. Sometimes that will require hard work, absolutely. But it should also involve working smarter.

Technologies like AI are tools that can help us work smarter. They're not replacing the need for creativity or hard work; they're augmenting our abilities and allowing us to focus our efforts where they matter most.

A sculptor using power tools isn't cheating or making their art less valuable. They're using available tools to bring their vision to life more efficiently. The artistry is in the vision and the execution, not in the unnecessary struggle.

The same goes for writers using AI. The AI isn't writing the book for you. It's a tool to help you brainstorm, overcome writer's block, or handle some of the more mundane aspects of writing. The "soul" of the story – that all comes from you. The AI is just helping you get it out of your head and onto the page more efficiently.

Now, I'm not saying we should all become lazy bums who let AI do all the work. Far from it. The sweet spot is in combining smart work with hard work. Use tools and technologies to make the process more efficient, but still put in the effort to refine, perfect, and inject your unique voice into your art.

Remember, the hard work doesn't disappear when you use tools like AI. It just shifts. Instead of struggling with every word choice, you might spend more time fine-tuning the overall structure of your story. Instead of battling writer's block, you might invest more energy in developing complex, nuanced characters.

The end result? You're still working hard, but you're working hard on the aspects of art that truly matter, rather than getting bogged down in unnecessary difficulties.

A Call for Balance

So, to our friend Hard-work Harold and all the other art hardliners out there, I say this: Let's not confuse difficulty with value. Hard work is admirable, but unnecessary struggle isn't a virtue.

Instead of insisting that art should be hard, let's focus on making art that matters. Let's use every tool at our disposal to bring our visions to life. Let's work smart *and* hard, combining efficiency with effort to create something truly remarkable.

We can still work hard, because hard work will always be important. But working smarter is better than working harder, and working smarter AND harder is the best of all.

30

"AI Removes the Human Element"

Now it's true that AI-text that had minimal human input does, at present, sound a little soulless.

That said, AI is only the worst it will ever be right now. It's going to get better, and you know what, there will come a time where it will be able to imitate what humans love so much, that one day you will probably be highly moved by something that AI wrote.

But thankfully we're not at that point yet.

But as I mentioned in a previous section: AI writing does not exist in a vacuum, it's a collaborative process between the human and the AI. And in that sense, it's just following the human's instructions. If the result is soulless, then that's the human's fault for not recognizing this, or not trying to correct it.

As always, AI is not meant to replace humans, but it's a productivity tool for humans to use to expand their own creativity.

It allows humans to take their own human element, that creative spark, and use technology to enhance it and strengthen it, much like other creative tools like Adobe Photoshop or the various VFX software tools can do, allowing us to do things that would not be possible without technology.

31

"I Do Fine Without AI and Don't Need It"

I hear this a lot from authors who say "I'm able to write fine without AI, so I don't need it, and neither should you."

This is a simple objection to answer.

First off, I'd like to establish that writing is a multi-step process, not just one activity, it includes (but is not limited to) the following:

- Brainstorming/daydreaming

- Plotting

- Character development

- Worldbuilding

- Troubleshooting story issues

- First draft writing

- Revision

- Developmental editing

- Line editing

- Proofreading

- Managing beta readers

- More revision

- Formatting/packaging

For the authors who say they don't need AI, they're most likely talking about writing the first draft. But let's also remember that AI can help at any stage of this process, not just writing the first draft. And it also doesn't have to be all or nothing.

As I'm writing this right now, I'm typing this out without AI. Sometimes when I know what words I want to say, I don't need AI at all and I can dive right in.

But there are other portions of these objections where I fed Claude a few ideas, and it gave me the first draft, which I then edited to my satisfaction. So it's not either or.

You Do You

It's absolutely fine if you don't want to use AI for any or all parts of the writing process.

HOWEVER, it's another thing entirely to say that other people should do it. Because not every author is like you. In fact, no author is like you.

Authors struggle with different areas of the writing process for a plethora of reasons: burnout, neurodivergence, ADHD, dyslexia, you name it. You can't assume that just because you don't need AI, that other people don't. There are people coming into the industry now that were *never* able to write a book or succeed in publishing before AI. That's amazing! AI is lifting the barrier to entry, and therefore, the privilege that writing affords people.

This is why I never criticize how and why someone uses AI. For instance, I get a lot of people who say that AI is fine for brainstorming, but not for writing the first draft.

No.

AI is great for wherever you need it most. Period. Full stop.

If you don't need/want it at all, good for you.

If you need it at every stage of the process, good for you too.

But find where it can help the most (if any) and let it help you in that area. Then spend the rest of your time on the other aspects of writing that you love the most, which you now have more time to work on, thanks to AI.

None of us should dictate how or when these technologies should be used.

"AI Can't Write Original Content"

This is another one that's easy to answer, because it's actually true.

But it's true in the same way that it's impossible for *humans* to write original content as well.

You see, each of us is a product of our experiences, our education, and the media we consume. Everything we create is, in some way, a remix or reinterpretation of what we've been exposed to. As the saying goes, "There's nothing new under the sun."

AI works in the same way.

It's trained on existing data, just like we are. It learns patterns, styles, and concepts from this data, much like how we learn from reading books, watching movies, or living life. When it generates content, it's combining and remixing these learned patterns in new ways.

But here's the kicker: AI can actually create more "original" content than humans in some ways. Why? Because it can process and combine information from a much broader range of sources than any single human could in a lifetime.

What people usually mean when they want something "original" is that they want something fresh. Something that combines two un-original ideas in a way that *feels* new. And this is actually something AI is very good at...

You Can Provide the "Originality"

Now I've created plenty of completely original content with AI. That's because I was the human guiding the AI. I gave it the outline of a scene that I wanted to write, complete with information on my characters and what I want to happen, and it created the first draft of the scene. That first draft has never existed before I prompted the AI to give it to me, nor will it likely ever get generated the exact same way again.

That's original content, folks.

It just requires a human to aid in the prompting.

Another story that I heard to illustrate this principle came from Joanna Penn in The Creative Penn Podcast. In one podcast that I was listening to, she mentioned that she used AI art for the cover of a short story. The short story in question involved an old mermaid. And she was unable to find any stock images of older mermaids anywhere. Most mermaids were young, and there just wasn't any licensable material that she could use to help make the cover.

But then she tried an AI art generated and prompted it to create an old mermaid, and she was quickly able to get something she wanted.

Now how can that be if the AI art generator wasn't trained on any old mermaids?

Easy. Because it's been trained on the mathematics of what older people look like, as well as what mermaids look like, and was able to combine the two ideas in a way that was completely original, because no one had done it yet, at least not in the way that Joanna Penn needed.

The key difference is in how we define "originality." If by original, we mean "never existed before in exactly this form," then sure, AI (and humans) can create original content all day long. Every time you ask ChatGPT a question, you're getting a unique response that's never existed before in that exact form.

But if by original we mean "completely divorced from any existing ideas or concepts," then no, AI can't do that. But neither can humans. We're all building on what came before us.

The truth is, originality isn't about coming up with ideas that have never existed before. It's about combining existing ideas in new and interesting ways. And that's something both humans and AI can do.

33

"AI Software Will "Steal" Your Documents"

So I see this concern a lot when it comes to specific software tools like Sudowrite or Novelcrafter. People are scared that if they use the AI in those tools, that their writing will somehow get hijacked to train the AI.

First off, let me put your mind at ease for those two programs. Because they're third-party programs, they don't collect any of that data, because they're not actually training any AI models, nor do they want to. This is true of pretty much any third-party AI tool.

However, some of the tools owned by the companies that make the models, such as ChatGPT or Claude's chatbot, do actually train their AI on some of the data that they get from the chats.

Now, personally, this doesn't bother me at all, because I know how AI works, and I know that it's highly unlikely that anything I write will end up in someone else's book in the exact same way. Because all that's happening is the AI is learning the mathematics of writing like it does when it's trained on anything.

In other words, go back and re-read my response to the objection that "AI Is Stealing Other People's Work," because all of the same principles from that response apply here: it doesn't matter if it's training on your work or not, because the odds of that becoming an issue for you, or for other authors/artists to "steal" your work is quite low.

Now, I will suggest you not put any sensitive information (such as social security numbers) into any of these chatbots, just in case, and because that's just good common sense.

But that doesn't mean that your writing is somehow in danger.

Additionally, if you're really worried about this happening, then some of the tools have paid plans that specifically state that your work will not be used in training. This is usually for more enterprise clients who have the aforementioned sensitive data that they want to feed into the AI for whatever reason (like automating certain business functions and such), but some tools like ChatGPT have this in all their paid plans (though you might have to turn the feature on).

I find it almost hypocritical of authors who are okay with AI using copyrighted books in their training dataset, but then somehow have an issue with these AI companies using your chats with their products to improve said products.

It's the same process, so if you're okay with one, you should be okay with the other.

And if you're not okay with either, well...see my first response to the "stealing" debate, and if that doesn't convince you, then I suppose we will just have to agree to disagree.

34

"AI Produces Plagiarized Content"

Let's tackle the thorny issue of AI and plagiarism, shall we? We've already talked about it a little in the first objection about AI "stealing" copyrighted material, but let's dig a little deeper.

First off, the likelihood of AI spontaneously spitting out plagiarized content is very low, especially for large sections of text. These models are designed to generate original content based on patterns they've learned, not to copy-paste existing work.

To get an AI to actually plagiarize anything more than a simple quote, you'd have to go out of your way to force it. And let's be real, if you're doing that, you're probably violating the terms of service of whatever AI platform you're using. So, congrats! You're now a rule-breaker twice over.

But here's the thing - we can't just throw our hands up and say, "Well, the AI won't do it on its own, so we're all good!" Nope. We've got to hold ourselves to certain standards when using these tools.

Think about it this way: I could easily use Adobe Photoshop to whip up an image of Pikachu dressed as Batman. Then if I tried to sell that image, I'm likely to get a "cease and desist" order faster than you can say "copyright infringement."

But in that case, it wasn't Adobe Photoshop's fault. It was mine.

The tool itself isn't the problem - it's how we choose to use it.

And that's why we have to focus more on the human in this case, rather than the AI.

For instance, what if you asked the AI to rewrite an existing essay for a school assignment? Sure, it might not show up on plagiarism detectors, but guess what? That's still considered plagiarism. You're just wearing a fancy AI disguise.

So while the AI itself is unlikely to accidentally plagiarize, humans can still find ways to misuse it. YOU are responsible for ensuring you behave ethically. The AI isn't going to be the one getting sued if you try to sell that Pikachu-as-Batman artwork. That's all on you, my friend.

Here are a few tips to keep you on the straight and narrow:

1. Don't pursue any "prompt hacks" that will somehow result in large chunks of plagiarized text. Not sure why you'd want to do that anyway, but just don't.

2. If you're using AI-generated content, review and edit it thoroughly. Make it your own.

3. Be transparent about your use of AI if required (like in academic settings).

4. Remember that AI is a tool to enhance your creativity, not replace it.

5. When in doubt, err on the side of caution. If something feels ethically iffy, it probably is.

At the end of the day, AI is here to stay. It's not going to replace human creativity, but it is going to change how we create. And that's okay! Just use it as the productivity-enhancing tool that it is, and we're golden.

35

"AI Is an Environmental Hazard"

Let me start by acknowledging this one, because concern for the environmental impact of these technologies is a valid one, and we should all be looking for better ways to improve these models so they have less of an impact on the environment.

And that impact is pretty substantial, with the energy requirements of big tech companies like Amazon and Google going through the roof, and one university's estimate that "ChatGPT consumes approximately 500 millilitres of water per interaction consisting of 5 to 50 questions," which includes indirect water usage.

However, for most of the authors I see using this argument, it's not because they actually care about the environmental impact of the models, they're just (once again) looking for excuses to validate their fear of AI. In other words, it's a false flag argument.

Here are a few reasons why this argument needs some work.

We Can't Point Fingers at AI Without a Lot of Other Things

If you're angry about the environmental impact of AI, you actually need to be angry at a LOT of other things in equal measure, otherwise you're a hypocrite.

For example, the amount of energy it takes to produce an image on an AI image generator like Midjourney is about the same as playing a video game for 30 seconds. Are you okay with video games?

Also, the amount of energy to chat with ChatGPT is about the same energy usage as scrolling through Facebook, minute for minute, and most of the authors I see talking about this concern are doing so on Facebook. Why is that okay?

And that's not to mention all other forms of cloud computing, cryptocurrency, using your personal phones and electronics, running your bank, powering your car, streaming movies, your heating and air conditioning, your dishwasher, and even when you take a shower. All of those things produce similar power levels as using AI, if not a lot more. We can't pick and choose which one is okay and which isn't, just from environmental impact alone.

Now don't get me wrong, ALL of these concerns are valid. We, as humans, have a big crisis with our energy consumption all around. And while clean energy negates these issues, it's still not cost effective enough (yet) to be the main source of energy for most companies.

But to point fingers at AI, when the rise of the Internet alone was SO much worse, is a bit of a flaw in your argument, and evidence that you're just cherry picking which energy usage is okay and which is not, just because you fear AI.

While it's important to be mindful of our energy use, it's also important to know that we actually can't do much all at once (not even the big companies can). We can only make small changes over time, and do things like improve the clean energy technologies so they're more cost effective, and therefore more likely to be adopted. Only through small progressive steps like these can we make real environmental change. We can't just stop all carbon emissions at once.

AI is Helping the Environment

The good news is, it's actually the very advancement of technology that is helping us find solutions to...the advancement of technology.

For instance, AI has already made HUGE leaps forward in fields like medicine and energy usage. In fact, scholars are saying that it's unlikely that the world will be able to meet their environmental goals *without* AI.

AI is able to do things that humans never could, like find more efficient ways to distribute power so there's no waste, unlocking breakthroughs in cold fusion, making the cost of producing clean energy tech more affordable (like solar panels, which actually take a LOT of energy to produce in the first place), and finding efficient ways to actually *reverse* global warming.

And given the advancements we've seen in medicine alone, it's only a matter of time before AI has the same impact on the environment.

Water Usage for Cooling is a False Flag

Some people point to the large amounts of water that it takes to cool AI data centers. Cooling big data centers like these is nothing new, but the requirements have increased since AI exploded onto the scene.

But the fallacy in this argument is that water cooling isn't using the water and then discarding it, launching it into space, or whatever people think happens to it. Usually there is a closed loop of some kind so the water can be used over and over again for the same purpose, or it goes through an extensive re-filtering process and put back into the local water system in ways that can often actually *improve* the quality of the water in the area.

I had one person I know point this out; she said that her husband worked for a foundry that made AMC chips, and they used multiple metric tons of water for cooling, and that all of that water was then purified and replaced, with frequent QA testing. In this person's case, it actually improved the water quality of the surrounding area.

And like I said, it's often a closed loop, where the water is used multiple times for cooling. In fact, I have one of those installed in my computer right now, a water cooling fan that uses water to remove the heat from my CPU, but I don't ever have to replace the water in that water fan, because it just keeps getting used over and over.

So water usage is not actually a good argument here.

LLMs Are Costing Less and Less

As with any technology, the efficiency of the product continues to climb as more money is invested in the product. And because of the profitability of AI at the moment, a lot of money is being invested into it.

That's why we've already seen a lot of new models that are just as efficient, or more so, than past models, and which cost far less to run (meaning they have lower energy requirements).

And these big-tech companies are *very* interested in lowering the energy costs of these models. Admittedly, this isn't necessarily out of concern for the environment (although I'm sure many employees of these tech companies do), but because every dollar saved is a dollar earned. If these AI companies can lower the costs of their models, they earn more, and that's an attractive outcome.

And they are succeeding, with the efficiency of every model getting better and better with each new release. Plus, as these models get better, people don't have to continue prompting them over and over to get the result they're looking for. Instead, people get the result right away, meaning they actually use the tools less for each task.

AI is More Efficient Than Humans

As it turns out, AI is actually far less carbon emitting than humans for the same tasks, according to a study from the University of Kansas.

In that study, the researchers compared the carbon emissions of a human creating an image or writing, then compared that to the carbon emissions of an AI doing the same tasks, and found that the AI had hundreds of times less carbon emissions.

This means that as we integrate AI to speed up some tasks that we, as humans, don't need or want to do, using these tools as the productivity tools that they are, we will actually be able to produce far more with less carbon emissions overall.

Now granted, we can't actually stop ourselves from having a carbon footprint, so that will exist regardless just by us continuing to live our lives. But at least we'll have more to show for our time here, and our human carbon emissions will be more efficient as a result.

36

"Writers Like to Write, so Why Use AI?"

This is a valid concern. Why would a writer want to use technology to replace the writing process if that writer truly loves writing? If you use AI, isn't that a sign that you don't love writing and therefore shouldn't be a writer?

What this argument fails to recognize, however, is that writing is a multi-step process. It's not just one thing.

I've mentioned this in a previous objection, but once again, here is a sample of all the different processes involved in book writing:

- Brainstorming/daydreaming

- Plotting

- Character development

- Worldbuilding

- Troubleshooting story issues

- First draft writing

- Revision

- Developmental editing

- Line editing

- Proofreading

- Managing beta readers

- More revision

- Formatting/packaging

And that's not even touching on all the processes around publishing and marketing that book, which is another entire list of things to take the author's time.

Notice that writing a first draft is only one option on this list, though most authors spend more time on the draft than they do on outlining or editing.

And most experienced authors will tell you that the key to good writing is not the writing, it's the editing, or if you hate editing, having a really solid outline to cut back on the amount of editing required.

I'd even argue that the first draft is the LEAST important part of this list.

In my experience working with authors, there is usually at least one process on this list that people don't like, even if they adore the draft-writing process.

THAT is where AI is useful, to lift you up where you hang down.

Figure out what your least favorite part of the process is, and use AI to make that part easier and higher quality.

And if you love to write the first draft, that's absolutely fine. Do that. Don't use AI for that part.

But I make a point of not prescribing how an author should use AI. Some people find the draft-writing part to be very difficult, and a huge choke point. To them I say, it's not all that important anyway if you spend a lot of time on outlining and/or revision, so if you enjoy those more, then use AI to get the draft out, and spend more time on the outlining/editing instead.

The point is, AI takes the drudgery out of the parts of the writing process you don't like, and gives you more time back to focus on what you do.

Think about it, if you were writing a film script, you're not also going to act in the film, edit the film, and master the sound too. Stick to what you're best at and let AI or other collaborators help you where you're weaker.

Additional Resources

Myth HQ, LLC

37

Everything AI Can Do For You

There are so many things that AI can do for you, and honestly, so many of them could not fit into this book. That's why I thought I would wrap this book up with a nice summary of every major aspect of the writing/marketing process that I could think of, where AI writing tools like ChatGPT, Claude, Novelcrafter, Sudowrite, etc. could be of help.

(Note that I'm specifically referring to the potential benefits of AI *writing* tools here. AI art, digitally narrated audiobooks, etc. and are not included.)

Pre-Writing:

1. **Idea Suggestions**: AI can generate a list of potential story ideas based on your input or preferred genre.

2. **Writing Prompts**: AI can provide creative prompts for just about any genre to kickstart your writing

session.

3. **Character Suggestions**: AI can suggest character archetypes or even specific traits and backgrounds.

4. **Character Profile Creation**: AI can help you create detailed character profiles, including personality traits, history, motivations, etc.

5. **Plot/Outline Suggestions**: AI can generate basic plot structures or even more detailed outlines to guide your writing.

6. **Subplot Suggestions**: AI can offer ideas for subplots that complement your main story arc.

7. **Theme Identification**: AI can help identify potential themes based on your story elements.

8. **Synopsis Writing**: AI can help you condense your story into a brief synopsis.

9. **Creating a Story Bible**: AI can assist in organizing all story elements into a comprehensive guide. You can even analyze a book entirely and extract story bible information from it.

10. **Worldbuilding**: AI can suggest settings, cultures, and even laws of physics in your story world. This works great with a good worldbuilding template.

11. **Query Letter**: AI can help draft a compelling query letter to send to publishers or agents.

12. **Mind Mapping**: AI can help organize your thoughts into a visual map.

13. **Fight Scene Choreography**: AI can suggest realistic fight sequences.

14. **Timeline Creation**: AI can help you create a timeline to keep track of events in your story.

15. **Extrapolation Assistant**: AI can help you explore the future implications of certain story elements.

Writing/Editing

1. **Writing!**: AI can assist in drafting content, from dialogue to descriptions.

2. **Fixing Grammar, Punctuation**: AI can automatically correct grammatical errors and punctuation.

3. **Text Analysis**: AI can provide insights into the readability and tone of your text.

4. **Descriptions/Show Don't Tell**: AI can help you improve your descriptive writing.

5. **Dialogue Improvements**: AI can suggest more nat-

ural or impactful dialogue.

6. **Autocomplete**: AI can predict and complete sentences for you.

7. **Poetry**: AI can assist in generating poetic lines or even full poems.

8. **Thesaurus**: AI can offer synonyms and antonyms to vary your vocabulary.

9. **Unique Styles**: AI can mimic different writing styles.

10. **Adapting to Screenplay**: AI can help adapt your story into a screenplay format.

11. **Adapting from a Screenplay:** AI can help you take a screenplay and adapt it to a novel format.

12. **Search for Most Common Words Used**: AI can analyze your text for word frequency.

13. **Conflict Suggestions**: AI can suggest areas where additional conflict could be introduced.

14. **Vocabulary Enhancement**: AI can suggest more advanced or varied vocabulary.

15. **Point of View Consistency**: AI can help maintain a consistent narrative perspective.

16. **Tense Consistency**: AI can flag and correct tense inconsistencies.

17. **Children's Book**: AI can help adapt your writing for a younger audience, and even write whole children's books.

18. **Comic Book**: AI can assist in drafting dialogue or descriptions for comic books.

Marketing

1. **Audience Identification**: AI can analyze data to identify your target audience.

2. **Title Ideas**: AI can generate catchy and relevant book titles.

3. **Description Generator**: AI can create compelling book descriptions.

4. **Audience Profile Interaction**: AI can simulate how different audience profiles might interact with your book.

5. **Keyword Ideas**: AI can suggest keywords for SEO and advertising.

6. **Email Headlines/Text**: AI can generate compelling

email headlines and content.

7. **Ad Headlines Ideas**: AI can create attention-grabbing ad headlines.

8. **Social Media Posts**: AI can draft posts to promote your book on social media.

9. **Hashtag Generation**: AI can generate relevant hashtags for social media promotion.

10. **Book Launch Plan**: AI can help outline a comprehensive book launch strategy.

11. **Author Bio**: AI can help you write a compelling author biography.

12. **Blog Post Generation**: AI can draft blog posts to promote your book or related topics.

13. **Recipes**: If your book is food-related, AI can generate recipes for promotional use, or even develop in-world recipes from your book.

14. **Audio/Video Sales Scripts**: AI can draft scripts for promotional audio or video.

15. **Meme Generation**: AI can suggest meme ideas for viral marketing.

16. **Merchandise Ideas**: AI can suggest merchandise

that complements your book.

17. **Outreach Emails**: AI can draft emails for outreach to reviewers or influencers.

18. **Press Releases**: AI can write press releases to announce your book launch.

19. **Optimize Title/Subtitle**: AI can suggest optimizations for your book's title and subtitle for better discoverability.

20. **Website Copy**: AI can generate copy for your author website.

21. **Branding Plan**: AI can help outline a branding strategy.

Learning

1. **Genre Explorer**: AI can provide insights into different genres and their conventions.

2. **Trope Identification**: AI can identify common tropes in your writing or suggest ones to use.

3. **Research Assistant**: AI can help gather and organize research materials. It's also good at extrapolating from research in a way that is helpful to authors.

4. **Writing Schedule**: AI can help you set and maintain a writing schedule.

5. **Writing Coach**: AI can provide ongoing feedback and encouragement.

6. **Analyze Your Style**: AI can analyze your writing style and offer suggestions for improvement.

7. **Analyze Another Author's Style**: AI can analyze the style of other authors for you to learn from.

8. **Review Analysis**: AI can summarize and analyze reviews of your book.

9. **Get Book Suggestions**: AI can recommend books for you to read, either for research or inspiration.

Other

1. **Bibliography Creation**: AI can automatically generate a bibliography based on your sources.

2. **Footnote Generation**: AI can help you create footnotes for citations.

3. **Dictation Clean Up**: AI can transcribe and clean up dictated text.

4. **Translation**: AI can translate your book into differ-

ent languages.

5. **Role Playing Game**: AI can help create scenarios or characters for role-playing games related to your book.

6. **Interact with Characters**: AI can simulate interactions with your book's characters for promotional or creative purposes.

7. **Copyright Page**: AI can generate a standard copyright page for your book.

8. **Image Ideas/Prompts**: AI can suggest image ideas or prompts for illustrations.

9. **Company/Imprint Names**: AI can generate names for a publishing company or imprint.

10. **Title Capitalization**: AI can correctly capitalize your title according to various style guides.

Final Thoughts

AI is a tool, and like any tool, it's good for specific purposes. But while it's very versatile, and can be used at almost every stage of the writing process, is probably *shouldn't* be used for everything.

When I started this journey, it was because I had experienced burnout, and found that AI really helped me get past some of my blocks.

But that doesn't mean I use AI for everything. Far from it. Outlining is my favorite step, for example, and I rarely use AI for that.

Likewise, I know authors who use AI for everything *except* writing prose, or who only use AI for brainstorming, marketing, editing, you name it.

A lot of the critics of AI seem to think that using it is an all-or-nothing deal: you're either an AI author or you're not.

The truth is a lot more nuanced, it's a spectrum.

So how and where should you use AI?

Wherever you need it most.

We all have a pain point in the writing process. Writing is a lot more than just sitting down to type out sentences. It's plotting, crafting characters, staring out the window for hours, it's choreography, psychology, science, and a whole lot of research. It's brainstorming, outlining, editing, and yes, it also involves typing out a few sentences.

We like to think of writing as one thing, but really, it's many.

And chances are, there's a part of that process that you enjoy less than all of the others. *That* is where you should start using AI, where you currently meet the most resistance.

I know you became a writer because there was at least one part of the process that you loved. And you deserve to spend more time on that process, and less time doing the other things.

That's why I firmly believe, with everything I have, that AI can and should be used by all writers. Not only can it help those who deal with a disability, ADHD, dyslexia, autism, you name it, but it can also help any author at any stage of the writing process.

So find what you enjoy most, and do more of that. Find what you enjoy the least, and let AI help.

38

THE TOOLS I USE

As an additional resource, I thought I'd list all of the tools I use for writing (AI and Non-AI). Note that some (not all) of these links are affiliate links, but as always I only recommend tools I personally use, and it costs you nothing extra.

AI Tools I Use

Novelcrafter

I believe Novelcrafter is hands-down the best fiction writing AI tool on the market right now. It tailors the whole AI writing process for fiction, specifically, and makes it simple, while also allowing for maximum flexibility. I use it for pretty much all of my books, even my nonfiction books, because it makes that process easier as well. I can't say enough good things about it, as of this writing at least.

Get it here: https://nerdynovelist.com/go/novelcrafter

Sudowrite

Sudowrite is similar to Novelcrafter and excels at making the writing process easier for those who struggle with prompting and don't want to learn. After using Sudowrite extensively, I can confidently recommend it as one of the top AI tool for writing fiction books and stories. That said, it's not my favorite pricing model, and its inability to incorporate some more advanced needs (like pulling in a fine-tuned model based on my own books, which Novelcrafter can do), is a big drawback for me.

Get it here: https://nerdynovelist.com/go/sudowrite

Claude

I found Claude to be an exceptional AI writing assistant that rivals ChatGPT in generating natural-sounding long-form content. It's prose is much more conversational and human sounding, and that combined with its long context window and generally great experience, makes it my go-to chatbot for most needs.

Get it here: https://nerdynovelist.com/go/claude

ChatGPT

I found ChatGPT to be uniquely suited for certain types of writing, especially nonfiction and steps of the process requiring structure. However, as of recently I've stopped using it due to the fact that most of its stronger features are available through the free plan, meaning I don't actually need the paid plan anymore. But that could change with future releases.

Get it here: https://nerdynovelist.com/go/chatgpt

Midjourney

Midjourney is my go-to choice for AI Art. While it's not the only tool out there (Leonardo.AI and Ideogram are also worth a look), Midjourney is still, I believe, the best tool out there authors who want to use AI art. It consistently produces the best-quality images with the least amount of skill required for prompt engineering, and it's what I use for interior artwork for my books, concept art, some YouTube thumbnails, and even the occasional book cover.

Get it here: https://nerdynovelist.com/go/midjourney

ElevenLabs

ElevenLabs is currently the industry leader in AI-generated audio. While not super cheap, the voices are often so real that many readers can't tell a difference, and it's still a lot cheaper than hiring an audiobook narrator. If you can't afford a narrator, I'd recommend checking ElevenLabs out.

Get it here: https://nerdynovelist.com/go/elevenlabs

AutoCrit

AutoCrit is an analytical program that will look at your manuscript and compare it to other books in your genre for various potential concerns, like number of adverbs used, instances of passive voice, sentence pacing, etc. It also has some major AI analysis tools which I find are super helpful for understanding your manuscript from a developmental editing perspective. In fact, I'd even go so far as to name AutoCrit as (currently) the best tool for developmental analysis of a book using AI, which is not easy to do. If you use this link below, you can actually get the lifetime subscription, which is way cheaper than going month to month.

Get it here: https://nerdynovelist.com/go/autocritlifetime

ProWritingAid

ProWritingAid is a different kind of AI program, focusing specifically on proofreading. The grammar checker catches errors, while tools like Word Explorer and Rephrase help me improve my writing style and sentence flow. The breadth of writing reports surpasses competitors, pinpointing issues from pacing to dialogue tags. While not a substitute for a human editor, ProWritingAid has become an indispensable aid for improving my writing and catching technical errors. For long-form writers on a budget, it handily beats Grammarly and similar software.

Get it here: https://nerdynovelist.com/go/prowritingaid

Non-AI Tools I Use

Atticus

Atticus offers professional book formatting capabilities for a fraction of competitors' costs. It's way better than other alternatives: cheaper, and available on all platforms (Windows, Mac, Linux, and Chromebook). Atticus has a lot of great features, including creating beautiful themes or choosing pre-made ones, effortlessly exporting ebooks and print books, and leveraging handy writing tools like spellcheck and word count tracking. And it's still being updated to become the ultimate all-in-one platform for writers. I use this for every single one of my books.

Get it here: https://nerdynovelist.com/go/atticus

Publisher Rocket

Publisher Rocket is a tool to do book market research, and to find the best keywords and categories for your book. Its keyword and competition analysis tools help authors optimize book discovery, while its category research uncovers lucrative niches and bestseller strategies. The software saves countless research hours by generating tailored keywords for ads and unveiling competitors' sales, rankings, and tactics. Plus, like Atticus, it comes at a lifetime pricing, so I no longer have to pay for updates.

Get it here: https://nerdynovelist.com/go/publisherrocket

Campfire

I was very impressed by Campfire and believe it is one of the best options for novelists who want to build out a story bible. Its standout flexible pricing model lets you pay only for the specific modules you need, from characters to maps and more. The software makes constructing your fictional world intuitive through guided article creation and relationship mapping. For authors seeking an uncomplicated way to organize and interconnect every element of their story world, Campfire is a superb choice that hand-holds you through the worldbuilding process.

Get it here: https://nerdynovelist.com/go/campfire

Other Recommendations

The Great Courses Plus

As a lifelong learner and mythology enthusiast, I was blown away by the breadth and quality of courses on The Great Courses Plus (formerly Wondrium). With over 8,000 lectures on topics from ancient history to writing fiction, it offers unparalleled access to foundational knowledge taught by top academics. I especially loved the mythology, King Arthur, and the fiction writing courses. Many authors need to take deep dives into random topics for their books, and I find The Great Courses Plus to be the perfect place to do that. Also, the How to Write Bestselling Fiction course by James Scott Bell is a must-watch.

Get it here: https://nerdynovelist.com/go/wondrium

Miblart

Miblart is where I go to buy book covers, almost every time. They're relatively inexpensive, especially for the quality that they provide. Plus they work in most genres, and even provided the cover for this book!

Get it here: https://nerdynovelist.com/go/miblart

Russell Brunson's Stuff

Russell Brunson is a personal hero of mine, and while many authors might not *think* his stuff is relevant for them, let me say that his information on marketing has been the backbone of my success. I model almost everything he tells me to do, in my YouTube channel, my books, my courses, etc. The best place to start learning is to read through his books, which you can get for free (+ shipping and handling) at these links:

- DotCom Secrets: https://nerdynovelist.com/go/dotcomsecrets

- Expert Secrets: https://nerdynovelist.com/go/expertsecrets

- Traffic Secrets: https://nerdynovelist.com/go/trafficsecrets

These are some of the only books that I own in all available formats (print, ebook, audiobook), because I use them in all sorts of situations, and I'm constantly reviewing them for tips to implement in my author business. I highly recommend.

About the Author

Jason is the man behind The Nerdy Novelist, a YouTube channel about helping authors write better and faster with AI. He is also the founder of Story Hacker, the premier system for helping authors write their first book with AI, and learn more about writing in the process. You can learn more about Story Hacker at StoryHacker.ai.

He is also the writer of many mythic fantasy books.

By day, he is the Content Manager for Kindlepreneur, and is living the dream within walking distance of the North Carolina beaches with his wife and daughter.

When he's not writing, his favorite hobbies include hiking, reading outside in his lawn chair, spending time with his family, and developing his websites.

The YouTube Channel

https://www.youtube.com/@thenerdynovelist

The Story Hacker Secrets

StoryHacker.ai

The Website

https://nerdynovelist.com

Nerdy Novelist Discord

https://nerdynovelist.com/go/discord

ALSO BY JASON HAMILTON

Roots of Creation

A New Light (short story)

Out of Shadow

Growing Ripples

Through Fire

Into Storm

To World's Above

As Winter Spawns

Seeds of Hope

In Creation's Heart

The Faerie Queen

Path of the Dragon

Lair of the Siren

Rage of the Beast

Strength of the Heroes

Fall of the Faerie

Rise of the Queen

Story Hacker Secrets

10,000 Words an Hour

From Zero to Published

The Plot Module